Dollars and Sense

Stay in the Black: Saving and Spending

Jeff Potash and John Heinbokel
Illustrations by Nathan Walker

1st Edition

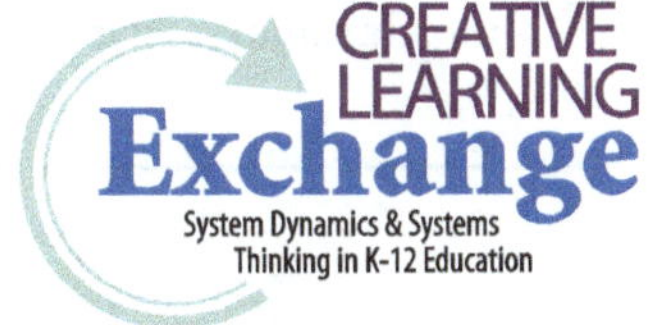

Creative Learning Exchange
Acton, Massachusetts
2011

DEDICATION

From Mitch Julis of the Julis Foundation

My enthusiastic support for this project is in loving memory of my father Maurice Ralph Julis and in honor of my mother Thelma Rabinowitz Julis.

My parents were inspirational teachers throughout their careers in New York with a strong interest in finance and economics. I am sure they would have embraced this book with great enthusiasm.

Dollars and Sense

Graphic Design/Layout: Amanda Wait, www.MiceSentiments.com

Illustrations: Nathan Walker, www.NathanWalker.net

ISBN: 978-0-9960128-0-5

Additional copies are available from:
amazon.com

Additional information available at:
www.clexchange.org

Printed in USA by Kindle Direct Publishing

Table of Contents: Dollars and Sense

Preface

The curriculum on Personal Finance, presented here, is especially timely after the global economic collapse of 2008, which provided powerful evidence that traditional economic and economic-educational thinking had failed. Our students' need for broad-based financial literacy has never been greater. In developing an understanding of how the pieces of our economic system work together, students should start with a deepened understanding of their own finances. This set of lessons focuses on core saving and spending systems that shape the outcomes of personal financial decisions. Future modules will link these saving and spending concepts with other important elements of personal finance (investment, credit, debt, and human capital).

This book, ***Dollars and Sense***, is the third in a series of curricula published by the Creative Learning Exchange (CLE), all of which utilize the tools of system dynamics to help students and teachers understand change over time. The first two books, ***The Shape of Change*** and ***The Shape of Change: Stocks and Flows***, by Rob Quaden, Alan Ticotsky, and Debra Lyneis, have been reprinted in a single volume, available from the Creative Learning Exchange.

Acknowledgements

The authors gratefully acknowledge valuable input from master teachers Alan Ticotsky, Rob Quaden (authors of ***The Shape of Change*** and ***The Shape of Change: Stocks and Flows***), Kelly Thieret, Bill Brakeley, Jane Potash, and the editing expertise of Willow Reed.

Funding for this first Module of Personal Finance and Economics was made possible through the generosity of the Julis Foundation and the Gordon Brown Fund.

Thank you all for making this project possible.

Dollars and Sense

Stay in the Black: Saving and Spending

Nothing is constant except change
Heraclitus of Ephesus (c. 535–475 BCE)

The materials provided here use systems thinking and mathematical tools and exploratory computer simulations to challenge students and teachers to develop a realistic and personal understanding of the dynamics of the economic system in which we live. With their resulting knowledge and understanding, they should be better able to control their financial futures, minimize the chance for future pain, and maximize the chance for fostering a prosperous future.

Personal finance, at its core, involves relatively few working parts. However, managing our finances is hard, because change is ever present and none of those parts ever stay the same for long. With money flowing in and out, our funds grow or shrink at different rates, at different times, and for different reasons. Without observing, analyzing, and understanding the patterns of change in money accumulations over time and without recognizing the connections that exist between all the parts of the system, adults frequently pay a real and heavy price.

As teachers, we can help our students prepare to deal with that critical but ever-changing system of personal finance. The innovative tools of *systems thinking* and *dynamic simulations* presented in these materials offer young students (5th–7th grade) a unique opportunity to develop a better understanding of the mathematics of change; to learn constructively and collaboratively;

and, over a lifetime, to successfully manage their personal finance. The activities in the seven lessons of this Module 1 utilize a series of computer simulations and their accompanying worksheets, which are designed to help young students explore how (and why) their personal finances change over time. As students explore the diverse set of financial situations, they will learn in four different ways.

- *Learn by doing (constructivism)*: asking open-ended "what if's" and using meaningful real-world examples.
- *Learn by building a conceptual foundation* that connects critically important mathematical tools (tables, graphs) and skills with a systems thinking conceptual framework that visually represents the dynamically changing financial systems (e.g., a personal savings account).
- *Learn by challenging preconceptions*, and using computer simulations to discover that there is more than one right answer or way to successfully manage one's finances.
- *Learn by sharing, comparing, collaborating, and applying lessons learned* to meaningful personal financial problems.

The core systems thinking building blocks that guide student understanding of the structure of change also drive the computer models underlying the simulations.

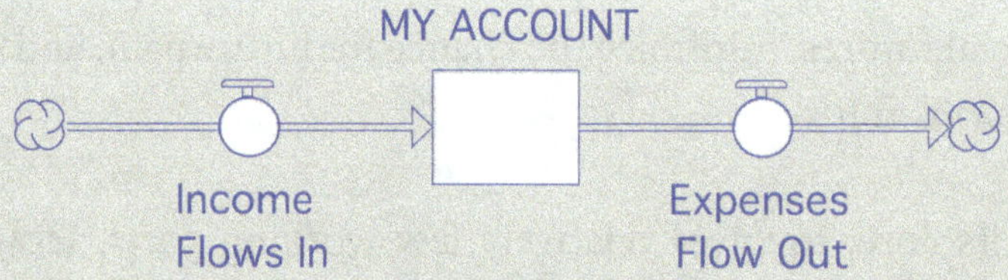

MY ACCOUNT

Income Flows In

Expenses Flow Out

- Money accumulates in MY ACCOUNT (we call that a "STOCK").
- An "inflow" into MY ACCOUNT—which can be wages, other deposits, or interest earned on the account—adds to that stock.
- An "outflow" from that stock—expenses—reduces or drains MY ACCOUNT.

The core message for success: Spend less than you earn!

Sounds simple, but when money flows in and out in different amounts and at different times… it is not nearly so simple! Yet our experience shows that 5th to 7th graders, working with mathematical tables, graphs, and computer simulations, can (and do!) "get it"!!

How Is This Module Organized?

Module 1 (Personal Finance) focuses on "saving" and "spending." (Subsequent modules will deal with investment and credit.) As in each module, Module 1 is open-ended. It allows for and encourages students to create and share mathematical approaches, tables, and graphs in order to explain and discuss personal finance goals, plans, and choices with peers, teachers, or parents. These activities are supported by the worksheets provided here and by the simulations that are available on-line.

Module 1 includes seven lessons, each of which contains a computer simulation with at least one challenge. The lessons are organized into three sections, each section progressively building on the foundations of the earlier section(s).

Section 1: Introduction to Personal Saving and Spending

Section 1 provides an introduction to linear (constant) saving, linear spending, and simultaneous saving and spending. We STRONGLY RECOMMEND it as a prerequisite for subsequent lessons.

- **Lesson 1: Can I Manage My Money and My Music?**

Section 2: Extended Saving and Spending Illustrations

Section 2 moves the understanding of simultaneous inflows and outflows forward by guiding students in choosing their own personal financial goals, running a business, operating a public service, or helping a friend plan to purchase a car. We provide simulations of each of these four illustrative scenarios.

- **Lesson 2: Can I Reach a Personal Saving and Spending Goal?**
- **Lesson 3: Can I Make Money with a Lemonade Stand?**
- **Lesson 4: Can I Successfully Run the Local Food Bank?**
- **Lesson 5: Can I Help a Responsible Teen Buy a Car?**

Section 3: Growing Savings through Interest and Compounding

In Section 3, the lessons move into compounding growth (rather than linear growth) to explore the role of interest on savings. We provide an introduction to compound interest and then a more ambitious illustration of long-term planning that brings together earning, spending, and saving with compounded interest.

- **Lesson 6: How Does Interest Grow My Savings?**
- **Lesson 7: Can Compounding Interest Make Me a Millionaire?**

Each individual lesson offers the following:

1. An open-ended and meaningful question or problem for the students to explore or solve.
2. Support for that learning through a set of System Dynamics conceptual and simulation tools to help students structure, improve, and communicate their understanding of these issues and processes.
3. Encouragement to expand that understanding by identifying and exploring "better questions" and other contexts in which those dynamics also apply.
4. The challenge and the tools with which to address problems of students' own creation.
5. Opportunities to share and communicate what they have learned with peers, teachers, and parents.

Frequently Asked Questions

? Will this be fun as well as educational?

Students love this approach. It is fun to play hands-on games and learn through experience. Students can work in teams, share ideas, talk with and listen to each other, not just respond to the teacher. Often something surprising happens and discovering the reason is eye-opening.

When students are active, cooperating, and solving their own problems, their level of engagement is high and the learning sticks with them. In addition, students who have struggled with more typical academic tasks often have a new opportunity to "show what they know" using new learning tools.

? Will this be complicated for me to teach?

Teachers are provided with concise supporting materials that include an overview and context for the student activities. Each lesson begins with a brief summary so that teachers can see what is covered. Background information is succinct and procedures are laid out step by step. Student worksheets are at the end of each lesson, ready to photocopy.

? Can my students actually do these lessons?

Although the activities in this book have been written with a focus on 5th–7th grade capabilities, they may be used with a wide range of student ages. Lesson 1 was designed to serve as a foundation for later lessons (2–6); those later lessons can be pursued in whatever way best suits the needs and interests of the teacher. Lesson 7 assumes the knowledge and understanding developed in Lesson 6.

What benefits do the students get from these lessons?

- *Students acquire new learning tools and work independently and together to apply them. Each individual lesson fosters constructivist learning.*
- *Teamwork gives rise to better thinking through dialogue, motivation to tackle tougher problems together, mutual respect, and fun.*
- *All the lessons are structured to build cooperative learning.*
- *Finally, each lesson is designed to provide practical opportunities for students to experience by doing, by making different choices, and by comparing and evaluating relative outcomes.*

How do these activities interact with recognized 5th–7th grade content and standards? (See also "Meeting Standards" table on page 7.)

The challenges presented in these activities take on big ideas that are central to the 5th–7th grade curriculum and that are transferable to other topics.

1. Module 1 lessons align with the National Council of Teachers of Mathematics (NCTM) Content AND Process Standards.

- *Content standards include skills for Number and Operations, Algebra, and Data Analysis and Probability.*
- *Process Standards apply to all areas (Problem Solving, Reasoning and Proof, Communication, Connections, and Representation).*

2. The lessons also address several of the Economics Standards advocated by the Council on Economic Education (CEE), including concepts involving opportunity costs; incentives; supply; demand; and price, interest, and earnings.

3. Finally, the lessons support the National Science Teachers Association (NSTA) standards related to the following:

- *Systems, order, and organization;*
- *Evidence, modes, and explanation; and*
- *Change, constancy, and measurement.*

Dollars and Sense

- Hands-on Activities
- Teamwork
- Reflection
- Dialogue among students
- Constructivism and inquiry
- Accommodation to different ability levels
- Sophisticated content
- High-level critical thinking
- Agreement with goals of national standards, e.g., NCTM, CEE, NSTA
- Simple preparation and easy directions

Curriculum Connections

The tool-sets and mind-sets developed here have application far beyond *just* an understanding of personal finance. As students use graphs to understand how money accumulations (STOCKS) change over time, they also find that similar patterns of behavior arise in other places in the real world. And their practical application of the systems thinking tools taught here to represent change can be applied to a wide variety of "systems," ranging from populations (of people, animals, plants, etc.) to resources and even to emotions about people and events. All of these systems in the real world are subject to factors that increase and decrease the overall STOCK in variable ways.

Meeting Standards

The simulations and worksheets that are part of each lesson are designed to use personal finance challenges to address age-appropriate CONTENT and PROCESS standards in Mathematics, as well as emerging national standards in Economics, the NSTA standards identified above, and the transferable tool- and mind-sets of System Dynamics that support wide-ranging critical thinking and collaborative skills. The following table provides a more detailed breakdown of how Module 1 relates to these standards.

Lesson	Math Standards (NCTM)	Economics Standards (CEE)	System Dynamics Objectives (CLE)
Lesson 1: Can I Manage My Money and My Music? Saving for a GOAL (an mp3 player and tunes), and spending "wisely" to make that savings last. ***Lesson 2:*** Can I Reach a Personal Saving and Spending Goal? Pursuing saving and spending PLANS to reach a personal goal. ***Lesson 3:*** Can I Make Money with a Lemonade Stand? Running a business, with income, expenditures, and profit. ***Lesson 4:*** Can I Successfully Run the Local Food Bank? A non-profit maximizing the "good" it does (rather than profits!) while needing to be sustainable. ***Lesson 5:*** Can I Help a Responsible Teen Buy a Car? Role of "trade-offs" (short-term vs. long-term gratification, sacrificing free time for work) to pursue a "big" financial goal. ***Lesson 6:*** How Does Interest Grow My Savings? Introducing the "miracle" of compound interest and its power for generating long-term savings. ***Lesson 7:*** Can Compounding Interest Make Me a Millionaire? Putting all of the pieces together—saving, spending, and earning interest—to see if an "average" person can become a millionaire!	CONTENT STANDARDS Number and Operations • Understand meanings of operations and how they relate to one another. Algebra (includes some Grade 6–8 standards) • Understand patterns, relations, and functions. • Use mathematical models to represent and understand quantitative relationships. • Analyze change in various contexts. Data Analysis and Probability • Formulate questions that can be addressed with data; collect, organize, and display relevant data to answer questions. • Develop and evaluate inferences and predictions that are based on data. PROCESS STANDARDS Problem Solving: Build new mathematical knowledge; apply/adapt a variety of strategies to solve problems; reflect on process. Reasoning and Proof: Make/ investigate mathematical conjectures; develop/evaluate mathematical arguments; use various types of reasoning and methods of proof. Communication: Organize and consolidate thinking; communicate coherently and clearly to peers, teachers, and others; analyze and evaluate thinking/strategies of others. Connections: Recognize and use connections among mathematical ideas; recognize and apply mathematics in contexts outside of mathematics. Representation: Create/use representations to organize, record, and communicate mathematical ideas and to model and interpret physical, social, and mathematical phenomena.	Standard 1: Students will identify what they gain and what they give up when they make choices. Standard 2: Students will make effective decisions as consumers, producers, savers, investors, and citizens. Standard 3: Students will evaluate methods of allocating goods and services, by comparing the benefits and costs of each method. Standard 4: Students will identify incentives that affect people's behavior and explain how incentives affect their own behavior. Standard 8: Students will predict how prices change when the number of buyers or sellers in a market changes. Standard 12: Students will explain situations in which they pay or receive interest. Standard 13: Students will predict future earnings.	1. Systems are dynamic, meaning that they are characterized by change over time (familiarity with Behavior-over-Time Graphs). 2. Dynamics in systems are a result of the interaction of stocks and flows (ability to create a simple one-stock stock/flow diagram). 3. Altering inflows and outflows can create many patterns of change in stocks (understanding different graph patterns and the underlying data and dynamics to which they are linked). 4. Inflows and/or outflows are controlled in many ways to achieve a desired size of stock (ability to manipulate a simple one-stock model to achieve desired outcomes). 5. Reinforcing feedback loops (e.g., compound interest) are powerful and often non-intuitive in their effects (familiarity with the concept of reinforcing feedback and how it influences stocks and flows).

Lesson 1

Can I Manage My Money and My Music?

Instructions for Teachers

Student Challenge:

Use a computer simulation to test different Saving then Spending plans to satisfy personal music needs: purchase of new Mp3 player and tunes over a 24-month period without running out of money!

At the Lesson's End:

- Students will have completed a structured exploration of how Saving and Spending combine to control their ability to achieve a financial GOAL.
- Students will have designed and tested a variety of PLANS for achieving that GOAL.
- Students will have used tables, graphs, and systems thinking concepts to share their results with classmates by doing the following:
  - Comparing successful (and unsuccessful!) PLANS, and
  - Exploring the different personal values that they, and other students, brought to this challenge.

(See the following Instructions and the Worksheets for more details.)

MATERIALS

- Computer Simulation (available on-line at http://clexchange.org/curriculum/dollarsandsense/lesson1.asp).
- Three worksheets (use as needed) to record plans and results.

Overview

Managing personal finances at any age involves setting a GOAL and then devising *and testing* a PLAN with two elements: Saving and Spending. For young students this learning is most powerful when they are provided hands-on opportunities to explore a system of saving followed by spending; to recognize and question their pre-conceptions; to specifically identify the choices they make; and to evaluate the outcomes from those choices. These elements of learning are illustrated in the provided computer simulation, which gives students a way to explore and tailor several different PLANS. The two parts of the simulation's Control Panel are reproduced below.

Inputs—Decisions

Can I Manage My Money and My Music?

You will need to make 4 Saving decisions for this simulation.

What is MY SAVINGS GOAL?

1) How much do I want to save BEFORE I start spending?

Savings GOAL

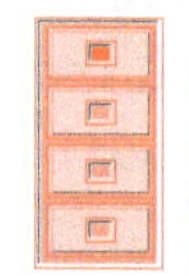

None
$100
$200
$300

Click a push button to select a Goal. A Green Light will show which is Active.

What is my Saving PLAN?

2) How often will I put (deposit) money into my Piggy Bank?
Click a button below.

Months Between Deposits

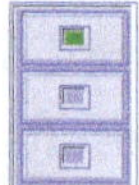

Every Month
Every 2 Months
Every 3 Months

3) How much will I deposit each time I set money aside?
Click a button below.

Regular Saving Amount

None
$5
$10
$15

4) Do you wish to keep saving, after you reach your Savings GOAL?

If so, click Button.

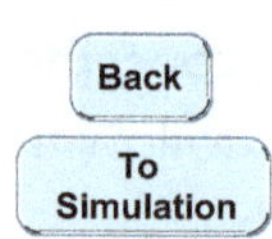

Outputs—Results

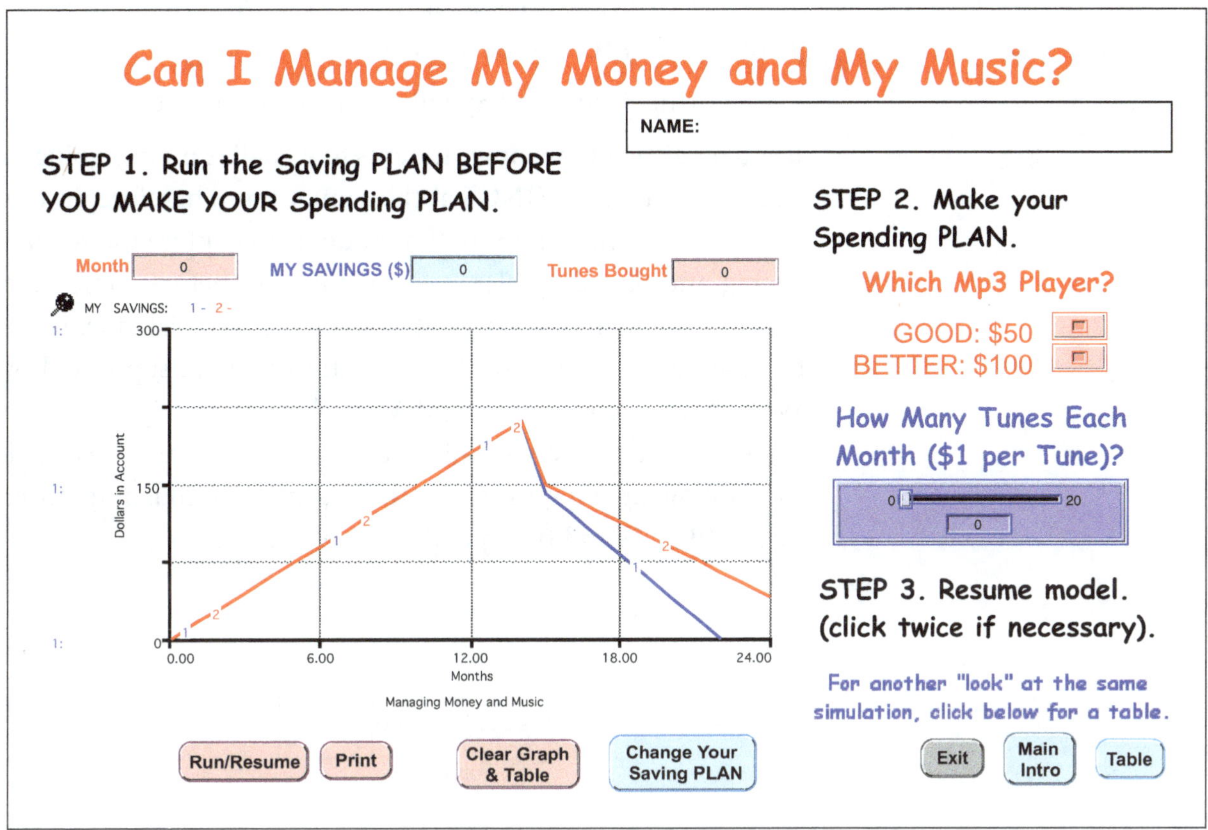

To more fully understand what is happening over time and why, these PLANS reflect the following system concepts.

1. Money (Saving) flows into the STOCK of MY SAVINGS, causing that STOCK to grow; and
2. Money (Spending) flows out of the STOCK of MY SAVINGS, causing the STOCK to decline.

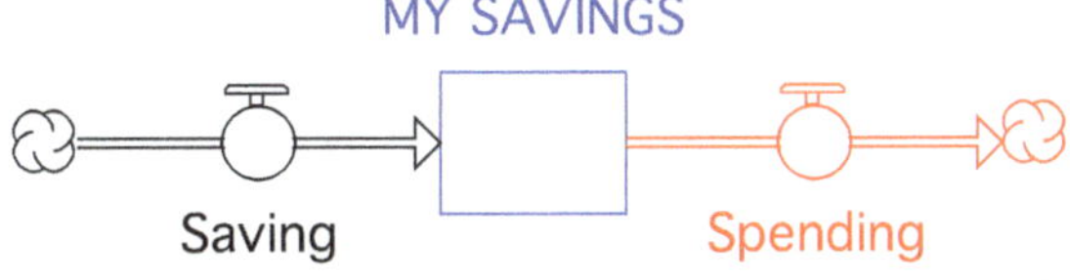

And, where both spending and saving are happening at the same time (as in the real world!), the GOAL for successfully managing MY SAVINGS over time is this:

Spend Less Than You Earn.

Lesson Structure

1. Exploring the Saving/Spending Financial System with the Computer Simulation

Exploring Saving and Spending in Isolation (optional)

It can be difficult for some students to visualize money going in and out of their SAVINGS at the same time. Therefore, in this lesson we provide an option for students to explore the regular Saving and Spending elements in isolation, before combining them in the main challenge of Lesson 1. The isolated explorations are accessible from the simulation and are supported by Worksheet A, for Saving, and Worksheet B, for Spending. In these optional exercises, only a 12-month time period is used. The following Graphs from the simulation illustrate three saving PLANS and two spending PLANS.

A. Saving

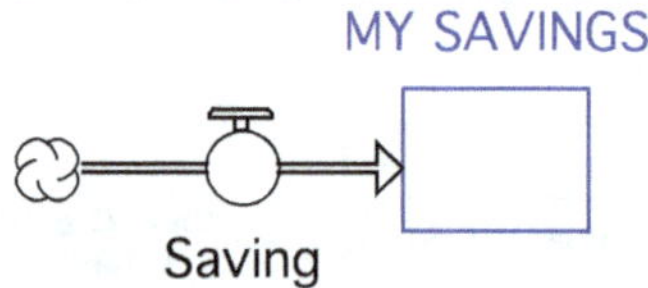

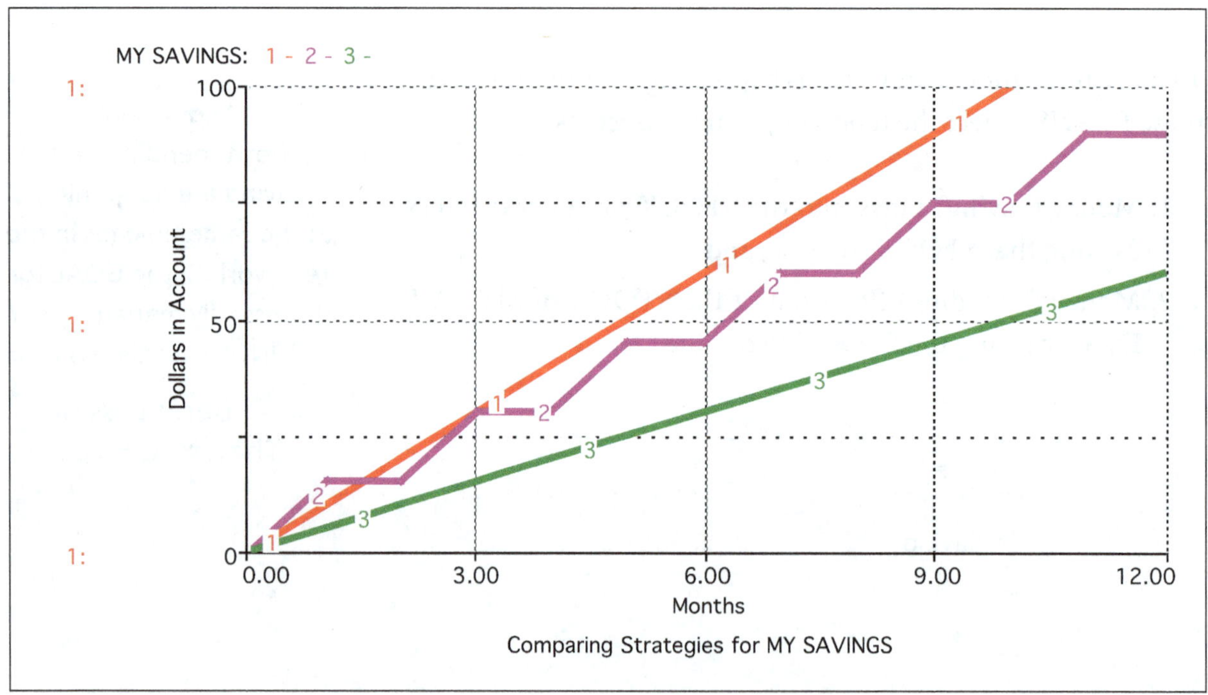

Comparing Strategies for MY SAVINGS

B. Spending

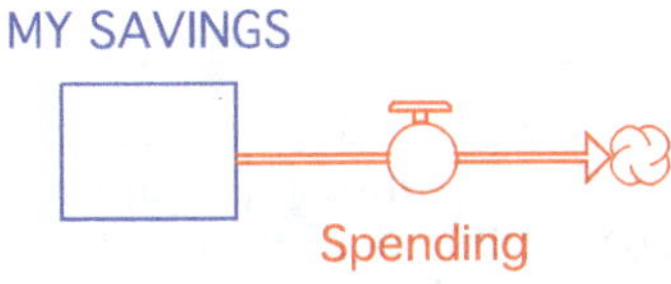

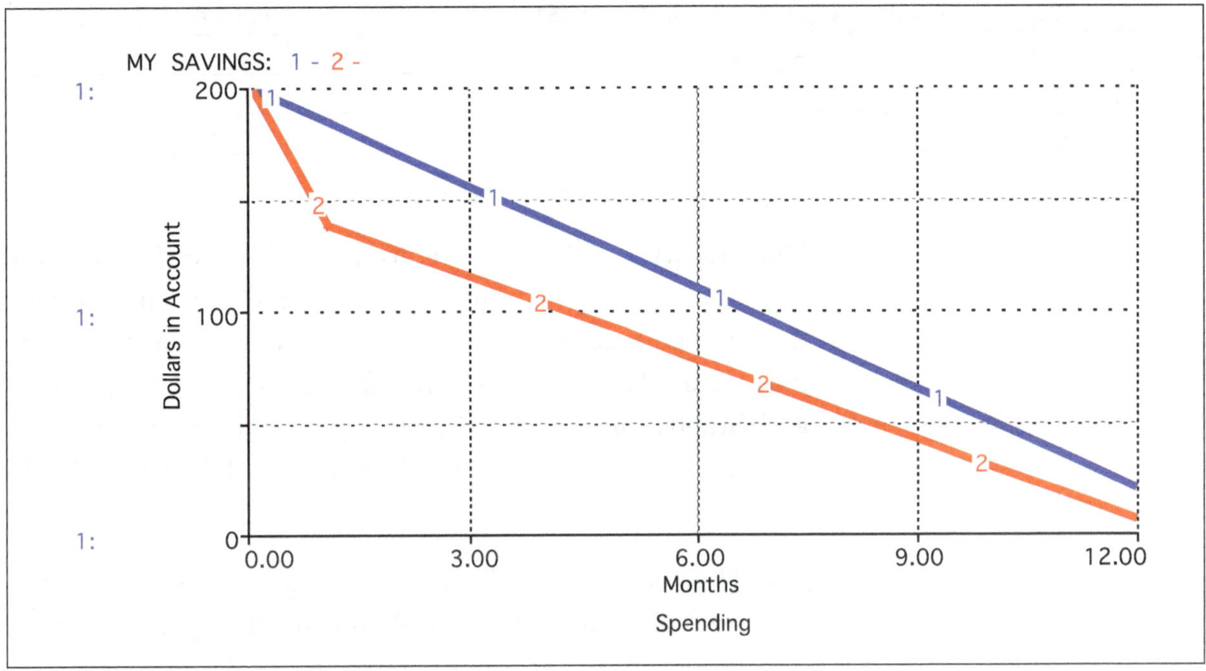

2. Making a Plan and Observing Outcomes—The Main Exploration

To engage students, Lesson 1 offers meaningful and open-ended questions for which there are many correct answers. Each student is asked the following in the simulation. What is your GOAL for satisfying your music wants? Can you devise financial PLANS for Saving and then Spending to achieve that GOAL? Finally, how do you choose your favorite PLAN? Worksheet C records students' decisions and their results as they explore different plans. The following Table illustrates some possible plans. The blank Table, ready to be filled in, is part of Worksheet C.

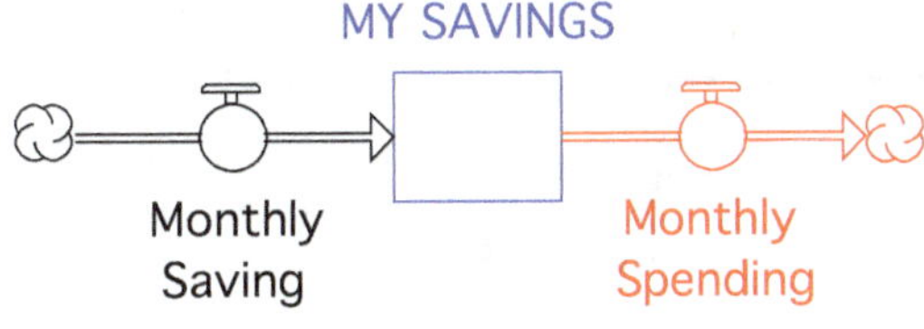

3. Recording at least TWO (or even three) Successful Plans

Your Choices							Your Results	
PLAN #	GOAL ($) (100, 200, 300)	Months Between Deposits	Saving Amount ($5, $10, or $15)	Cost of MP3 Player ($50,$100)	Tunes Purchased Monthly ($1/tune)	Continue to Save After Reach GOAL?	Total Tunes Purchased	Final MY SAVINGS ($)
1	200	1	10	100	15	N	60	40
2	100	2	15	50	10	Y	110	20
3	100	1	10	50	13	Y	182	8

4. Using Graphs and Tables

Students will work with Graphs and Tables to describe and communicate the patterns of change that they observe over time in their accounts (with those accounts first growing as savings accumulate to a GOAL, then falling with spending). Tables and Graphs can be printed from the simulation or created by the students themselves using Worksheet C. Tables and Graphs each have distinct strengths.

- The Behavior-over-Time Graph is designed to record multiple plans by focusing only on the changing amount of money in the account each month.

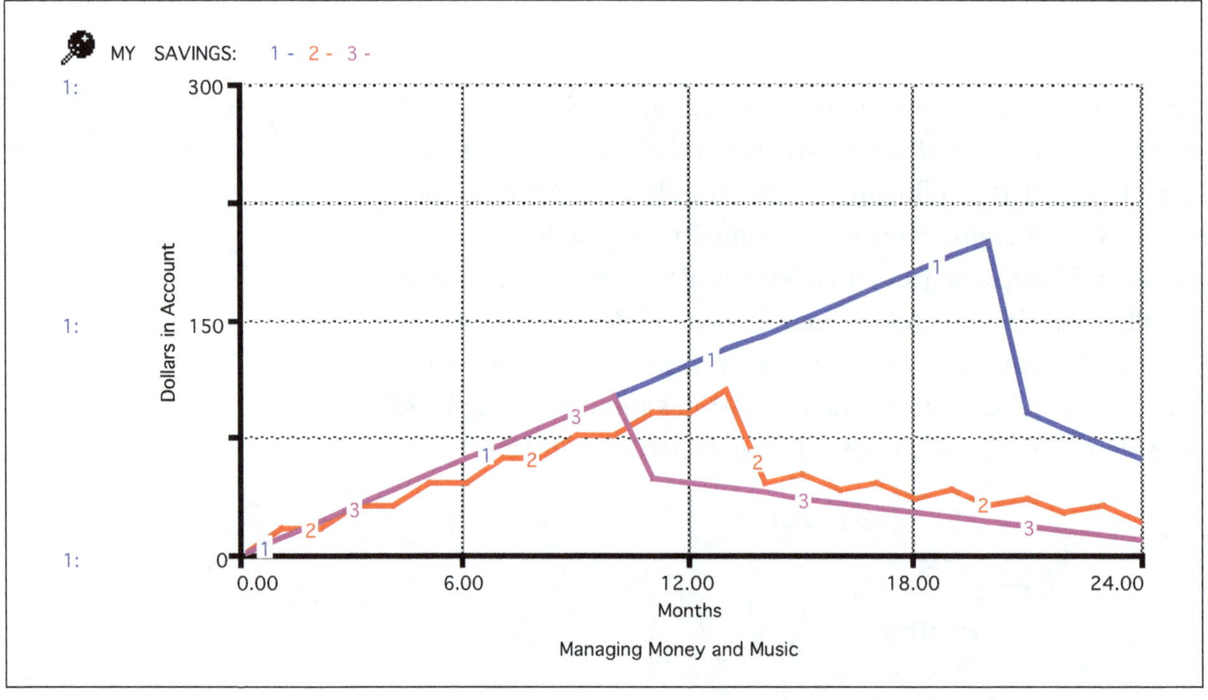

- A Table records monthly changes in money saved (inflow), money spent (outflow), and money in one's account (MY SAVINGS, the STOCK). That corresponds to the important Systems conceptual frame described earlier. The Table below shows the result of Plan 3 (shown above in Section 3).

Months	MY SAVINGS	Monthly Saving	Monthly Spending
0	0.00	10.00	0.00
1	10.00	10.00	0.00
2	20.00	10.00	0.00
3	30.00	10.00	0.00
4	40.00	10.00	0.00
5	50.00	10.00	0.00
6	60.00	10.00	0.00
7	70.00	10.00	0.00
8	80.00	10.00	0.00
9	90.00	10.00	0.00
10	100.00	10.00	63.00
11	47.00	10.00	13.00
12	44.00	10.00	13.00
13	41.00	10.00	13.00
14	38.00	10.00	13.00
15	35.00	10.00	13.00
16	32.00	10.00	13.00
17	29.00	10.00	13.00
18	26.00	10.00	13.00
19	23.00	10.00	13.00
20	20.00	10.00	13.00
21	17.00	10.00	13.00
22	14.00	10.00	13.00
23	11.00	10.00	13.00
Final	8.00		

5. Putting the Pieces Together

Students now ANALYZE and DESCRIBE what happened and why. This involves three steps:

1. Using a Graph to compare different options, recognizing that each student can devise more than one successful PLAN;

2. Using a Table to describe changes over time;
3. Finally, working and communicating with other students to compare observations and to recognize that individuals may make different choices based on different values (reflecting different desires or needs or priorities).

Where and When Will Students Need Guidance?

"Playing" on computers is second nature to students. However, they are likely to require assistance in the following areas.

Students record their PLANS without focusing on one "right" answer.

1. **Recording Data.** Computer games focus all too often on one dimension: "Winning." But in this lesson, we are asking students to record PLANS and to record the consequences of those specific plans without focusing on discovering the one "right" answer.
2. **Understanding WHYs.** Here, it may be appropriate to slow students down, and ask them initially to focus ONLY on their Saving PLAN or ONLY on their Spending PLAN. This simulation offers students an opportunity to do so, and Worksheets A and B provide you with a means to follow and evaluate student progress or problems with each of those financial elements and then with their combination into an overall plan. Even then (Worksheet C), students save first, then spend, so that they are able to recognize how each process affects the overall health of their accounts.
3. **Explanation of the structure of the tables produced by the STELLA® software.** The best way to read these tables is to recognize that the MY SAVINGS values for each month represent the *ending* value for that month. So for the Table above (in Section 4), beginning with month 14, we see that at *the end of month 14,* we have $38 saved. We then save $10 and spend $13, so that at *the end of month 15,* we now have $35 saved, a net reduction of $3 during that 15th month.

Bringing the Lesson Home

? How do the students set GOALS and define priorities—distinguishing NEEDS from WANTS?

One of the most valuable lessons in a financial literacy program is helping the students to recognize the difference between NEEDS and WANTS. That difference is especially critical when resources are limited. This lesson focuses on students' "wants." Later lessons will bring in a greater consideration of "needs" and the balancing that "needs" and "wants" often requires.

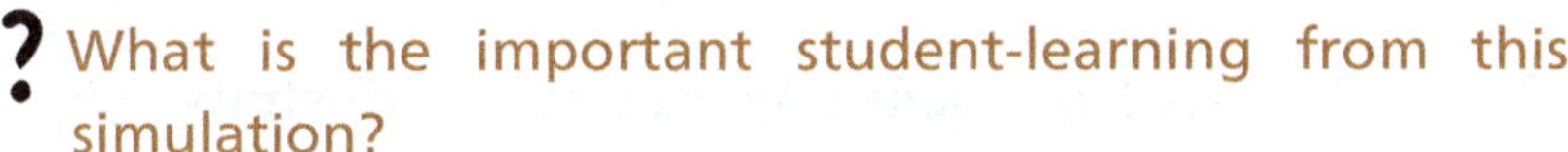

? What is the important student-learning from this simulation?

Appreciation of the importance of math in managing personal finance including the following:

1. *Success in using different strategies or plans.*
2. *Understanding the utility of Graphs and Tables.*
3. *Ability to apply the various tools in explaining their personal choices.*
    - *Ability to compare, discuss, and even (respectfully and constructively) disagree with each other on their choices.*
    - *Realization that learning can be powerful when listening and learning from each other.*
    - *Experiencing an open-ended opportunity for learning and discovering the empowering nature of such an experience.*

Extending the Learning

By providing students with more open-ended opportunities to create their own problem(s), they can learn to see and apply what they have learned to a personal scenario. This application is, of course, the most meaningful of all options. Lesson 2 offers such an opportunity.

Name____

Can a Regular Saving PLAN Build SAVINGS of $100 in 12 Months?

SAVINGS grow steadily when you maintain a regular saving program. **In this exercise, your GOAL is to pick a PLAN that will best allow YOU PERSONALLY to save $100 (or more) in your Piggy Bank in 12 months. A computer simulation will help you explore your options.**

You may choose: a. An amount of regular savings: ($5, $10, or $15); and
b. The number of months between deposits: (1, 2, or 3).

1. Use the simulation to test different PLANS. How many ways can you successfully save that $100?

Circle your successful PLANS below.

$5 Every Month	$5 Every 2 Months	$5 Every 3 Months
$10 Every Month	$10 Every 2 Months	$10 Every 3 Months
$15 Every Month	$15 Every 2 Months	$15 Every 3 Months

2. Then, pick the PLAN you like best and complete the Table and Graph on the following page.

***Instructions for Table*:**
Record, for each month you add to the Piggy Bank, how much ($5, $10, $15) you add in the "Regular Saving" column of the Table. (Record $0 for those months when you don't add anything.) Add the "Regular Saving" amount to the "MY SAVINGS" column for the next month. As an example, if you add $10 in Month 0, the "MY SAVINGS" box in Month 1 is $0 + $10 = $10.

Month #	MY SAVINGS	Regular Saving
0	$0	
1		
2		
3		
4		
5		
6		
7		
8		
9		
10		
11		
Final		

Instructions for Graph: Use either a Bar or Line Graph.

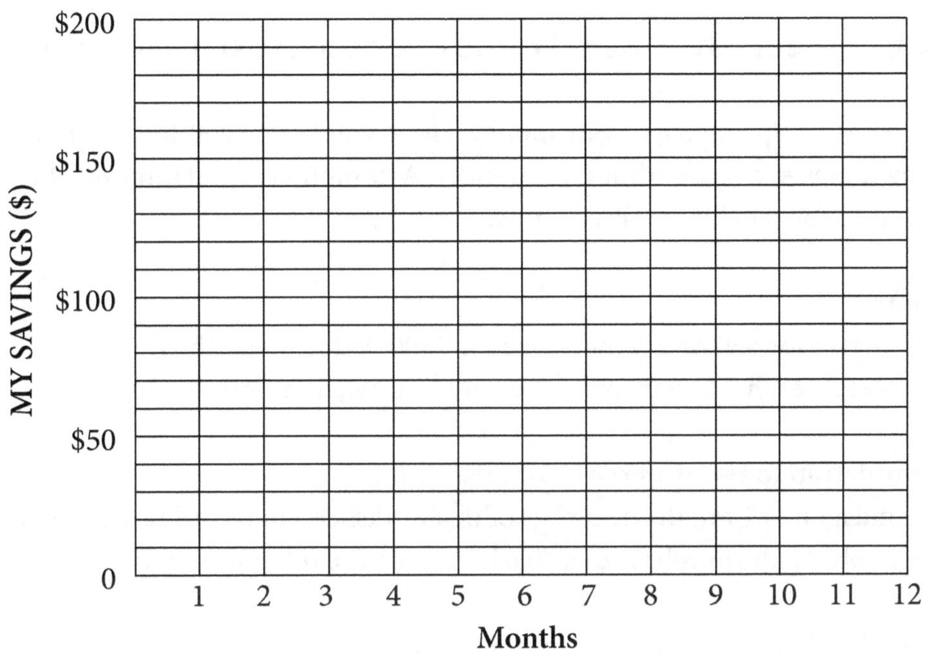

3. When you explain how your PLAN works to others, which visual representation helps you "see" better what is happening in your Piggy Bank—a Table or a Graph? Explain.

____

____

____

4. If you want to compare a different regular Saving PLAN (say, saving $9 a month), which would be easiest to use, a Table or a Graph? ______________________

Name____

Will My Gifts ($200) Meet My Music Wants over the Next 12 Months?

Developing a spending PLAN helps manage your money. Here, you have $200 to spend on a new Mp3 player and new tunes every month for 12 months. A computer simulation will help you understand your options for satisfying these "wants."

1. Consider your options.

- I can buy a "basic" player for $50 or a "fancy" one for $100. Which will I buy?
- Music downloads cost $1 each. How many do I want to buy each month (0–20)?

2. Use the computer simulation to test different PLANS.

Use a Graph (from the simulation or from the next page of this worksheet) to record two different, successful PLANS, one involving the purchase of a "basic" player, the other a "fancy" player.

3. Choose your favorite PLAN and record (on paper) its results using the Table below.

Month #	MY SAVINGS	Cost of Tunes	Mp3 Cost
0	$200		
1			---
2			---
3			---
4			---
5			---
6			---
7			---
8			---
9			---
10			---
11			---
Final		---	---

- Record your Mp3 player cost ($50 or $100) in the right column of the "0" line.
- Then record the cost of your music downloads in the "Cost of Tunes" column for each of the 12 months, beginning with the "0" line.
- Subtract each month's spending (tunes and Mp3 costs) from that month's starting amount in "MY SAVINGS." Enter that difference in the next month's "MY SAVINGS" box.

4. Use information from the Graph or Table to explain WHY you chose this Spending PLAN.

____

____

Will My Gifts ($200) Meet My Music Wants over the Next 12 Months?

Graph your PLAN (or PLANS) below.

PLAN 1 (Line 1):

Money in Piggy Bank at start __________

Tunes to purchase each month__________

Mp3 cost (at start) __________

PLAN 2 (Line 2):

Money in Piggy Bank at start __________

Tunes to purchase each month__________

Mp3 cost (at start) _________

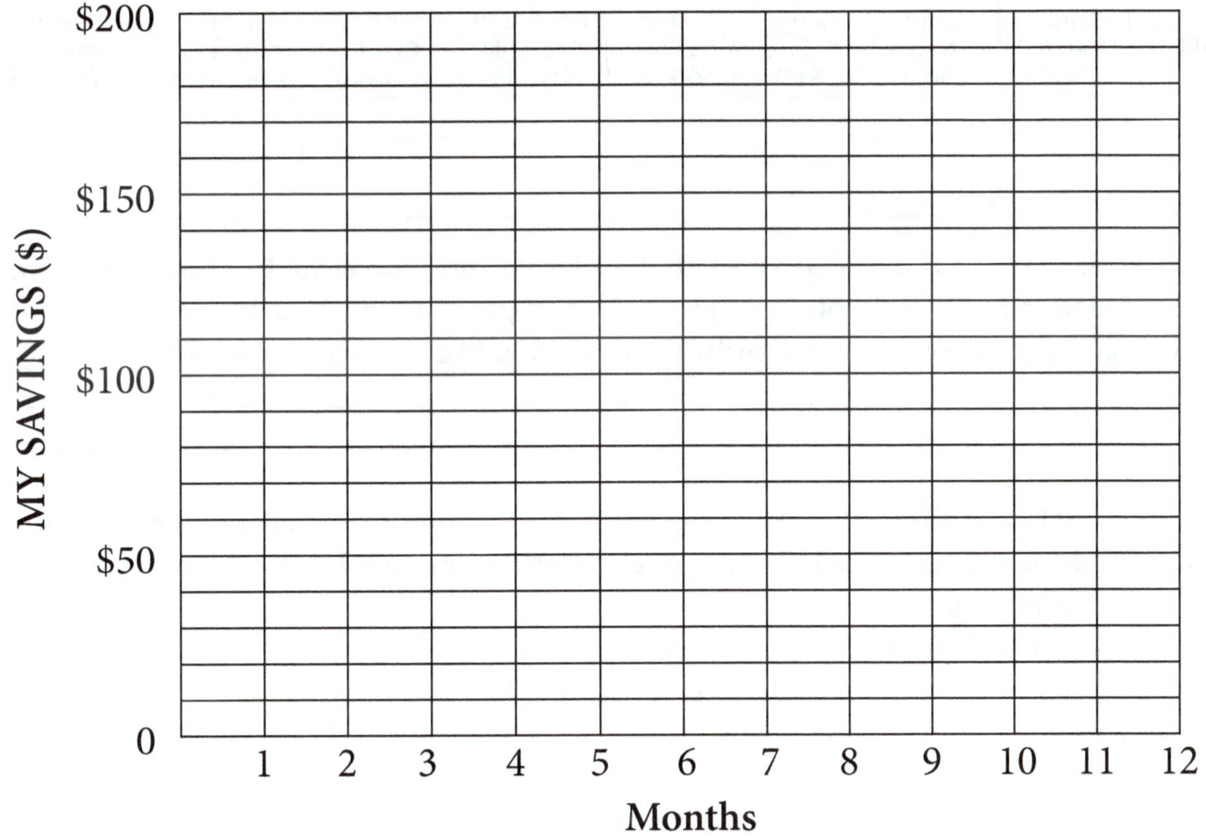

Name____

Can I Manage My Money and My Music?

You want to save enough money to then be able to buy an Mp3 player AND buy new tunes each month. Choose a Savings GOAL, then a Saving and Spending PLAN (see options in table below). **Test different PLANS with the computer simulation.** Identify the PLAN that best satisfies *your* personal money and music wants. Remember, there is no one "right" answer. However, your SAVINGS must last for 24 months, so that you can stay up to date with your tunes collection!

1. Record three successful PLANS below. These three PLANS are your possible "options."

Your Choices							Your Results	
PLAN #	GOAL ($) (100, 200, 300)	Months Between Deposits	Saving Amount ($5, $10, or $15)	Cost of Mp3 Player ($50,$100)	Tunes Purchased Monthly ($1/tune)	Continue to Save After Reach GOAL? (yes/no)	Total Tunes Purchased	Final MY SAVINGS ($)
1								
2								
3								

2. Next, use a Graph that shows MY SAVINGS $ for the three successful PLANS. (Print from the simulation or fill in the blank graph on the next page.) Each tells a different "story" of what was happening over time. Identify the PLAN you like best and explain *why* below.

____

____

3. Use a Table that shows the PLAN you chose. (Print from the simulation or fill in the blank Table on the next page.) Identify which months (for example, Months 1–6) you were doing the following:

A. Making *ONLY* Saving deposits ? Months ______ B. *ONLY* Spending? Months ______

C. *BOTH* making Saving deposits *AND* Spending? Months __________

D. *Increasing* MY SAVINGS? Months ______ E. *Decreasing* MY SAVINGS? Months ______

4. Use the Stock and Flow Diagram (shown to the right) to explain how the "system" works. (In the sentences below, insert "Saving" and "Spending" on the appropriate lines.)

A. MY SAVINGS will always increase when _______ is greater than __________.

B. MY SAVINGS will always decrease when _______ is greater than __________.

Optional Table and Graph (for recording results)

Months	MY SAVINGS	Monthly Saving	Monthly Spending
0			
1			
2			
3			
4			
5			
6			
7			
8			
9			
10			
11			
12			
13			
14			
15			
16			
17			
18			
19			
20			
21			
22			
23			
Final			

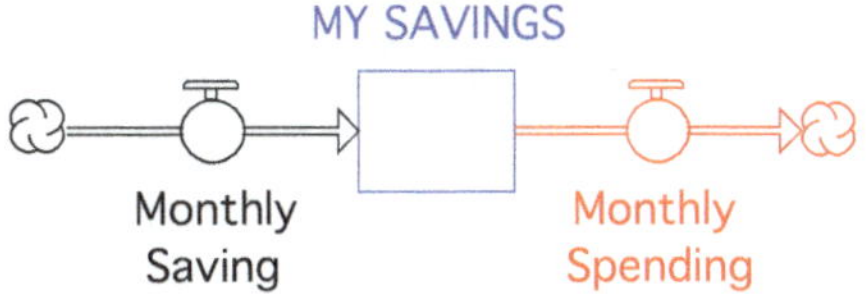

Use Table to record "Favorite" PLAN (using Information from Computer Simulation).

Use Graph to plot ALL successful PLANS.

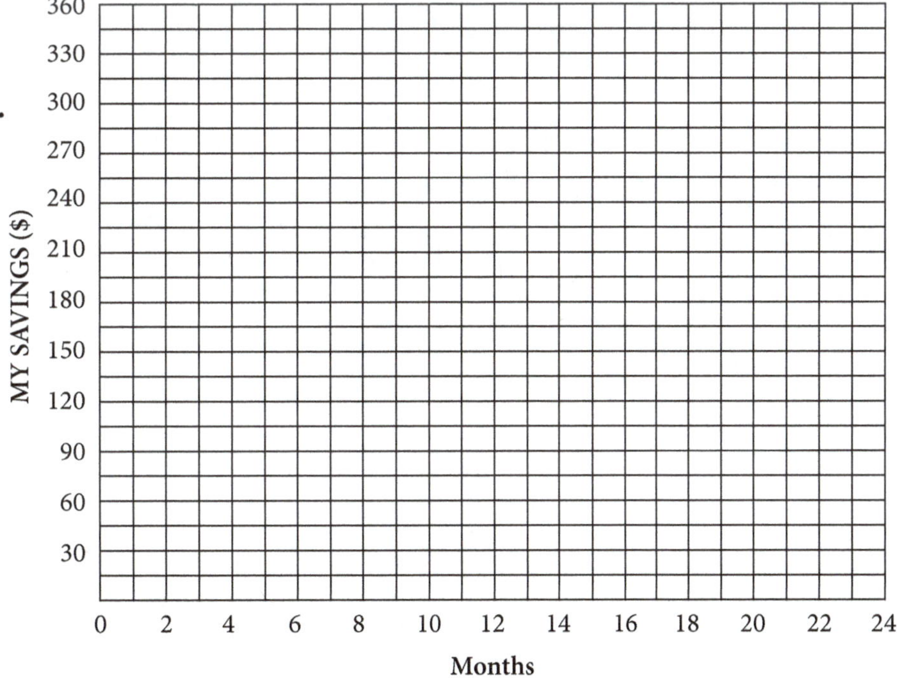

Lesson 2

Can I Reach a Personal Saving and Spending Goal?

Note:

The material developed in Lesson 1 is strongly recommended to familiarize students with the basic concepts that are used and further expanded in this lesson.

Instructions for Teachers

Student Challenge:

Identify a *personal* financial GOAL and use the simulation to test different Saving then Spending PLANS for achieving that GOAL within a 2-year (104 week) period.

At the Lesson's End:

- Students will have completed a structured exploration of how Saving and Spending combine to control their ability to achieve a personal financial GOAL.
- Students will have designed and tested a variety of PLANS for achieving that GOAL.
- Students will have used tables, graphs, and systems thinking concepts to share their results with classmates (and parents!) by doing the following:
  - Comparing successful (and unsuccessful!) PLANS, and
  - Exploring the underlying values they brought to this challenge.

(See the following Instructions and the Worksheets for more details.)

MATERIALS

- Computer Simulation (available on-line at http://clexchange.org/curriculum/dollarsandsense/lesson2.asp).
- Three worksheets (use as needed) to record plans and results.

Overview

As developed in Lesson 1, managing a personal plan involves setting a GOAL and then devising and testing a PLAN with two elements: Saving followed by Spending. Lesson 2 provides the opportunity for young students to select or "create" their own problem. This adds to the lesson's powerful hands-on learning that recognizes and challenges preconceptions, explicitly identifies choices, and evaluates outcomes. The simulation's Control Panel, reproduced below, illustrates how these learning elements are developed as students explore and tailor a variety of PLANS. Two PLANS are illustrated below: (1) \$5 weekly saving to a GOAL of \$200, followed by spending of \$3 per week; (2) \$5 weekly saving to a GOAL of \$300, followed by spending of \$5 per week.

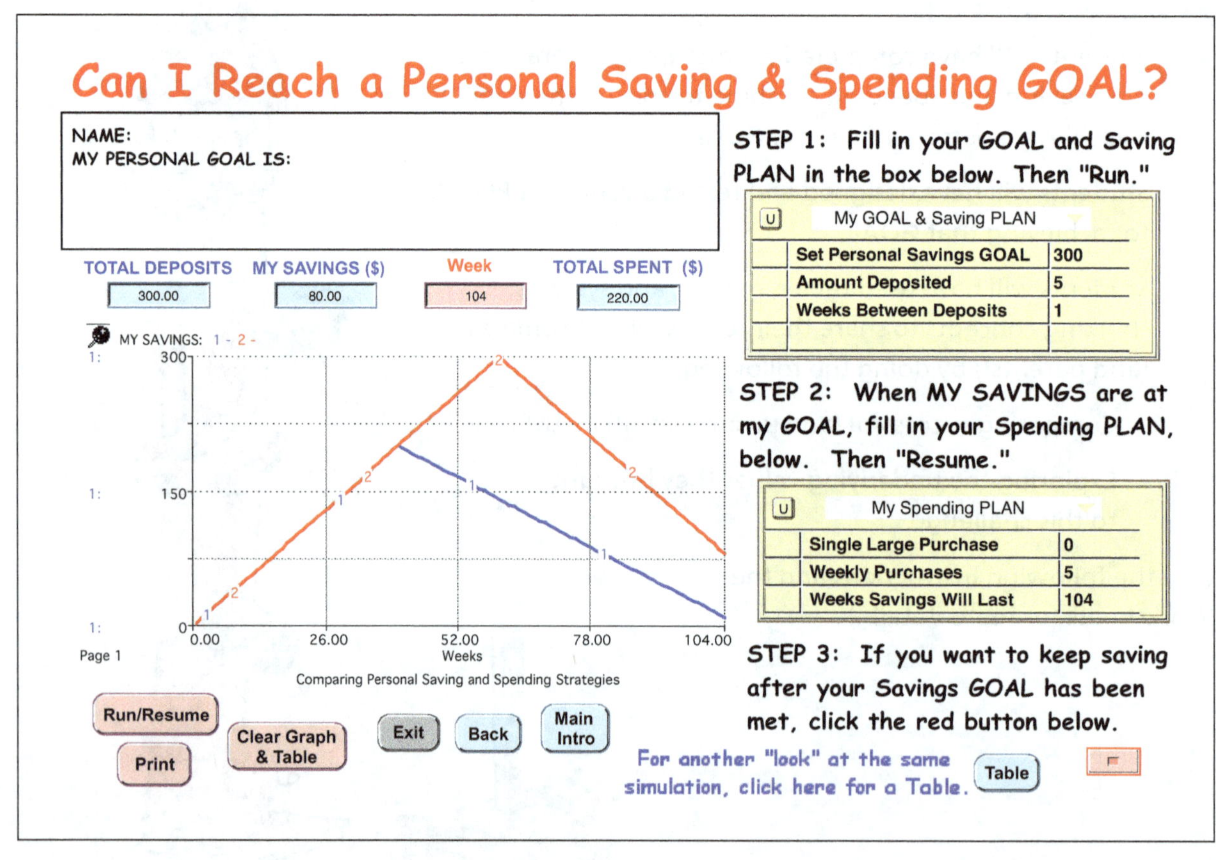

Two basic concepts are essential to fully understand what is happening over time, and why, in these financial systems.

1. Money (Saving) flows into the STOCK of MY SAVINGS, causing that STOCK to grow; and
2. Money (Spending) flows out of the STOCK of MY SAVINGS, causing the STOCK to decline.

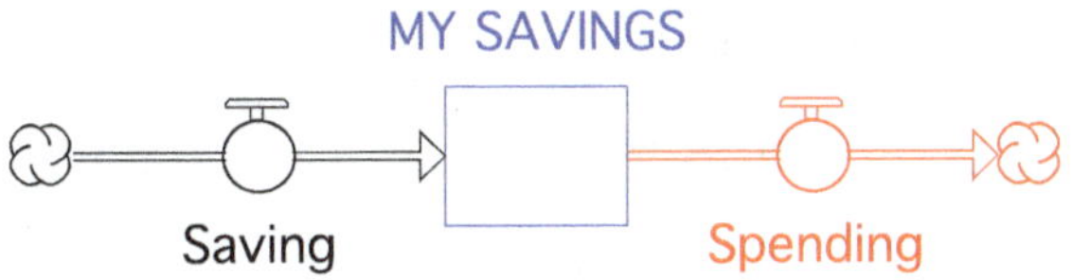

Lesson Structure

1. Exploring the Saving/Spending Financial System with the Simulation

Exploring Saving and Spending in Isolation (optional)

Some students may find it difficult to visualize money going in and out of their SAVINGS at the same time. Therefore, as in Lesson 1, we provide an option for students to explore the regular Saving and Spending elements in this lesson in isolation, before combining them in the main challenge of Lesson 2. These isolated explorations are accessible from the simulation and are supported by Worksheet A, for Saving, and Worksheet B, for Spending. (NOTE: these optional exercises run for a 52-week time period rather than the 12 months used in Lesson 1.)

A. Saving

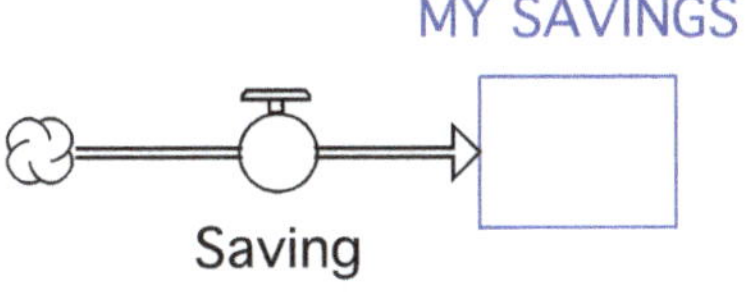

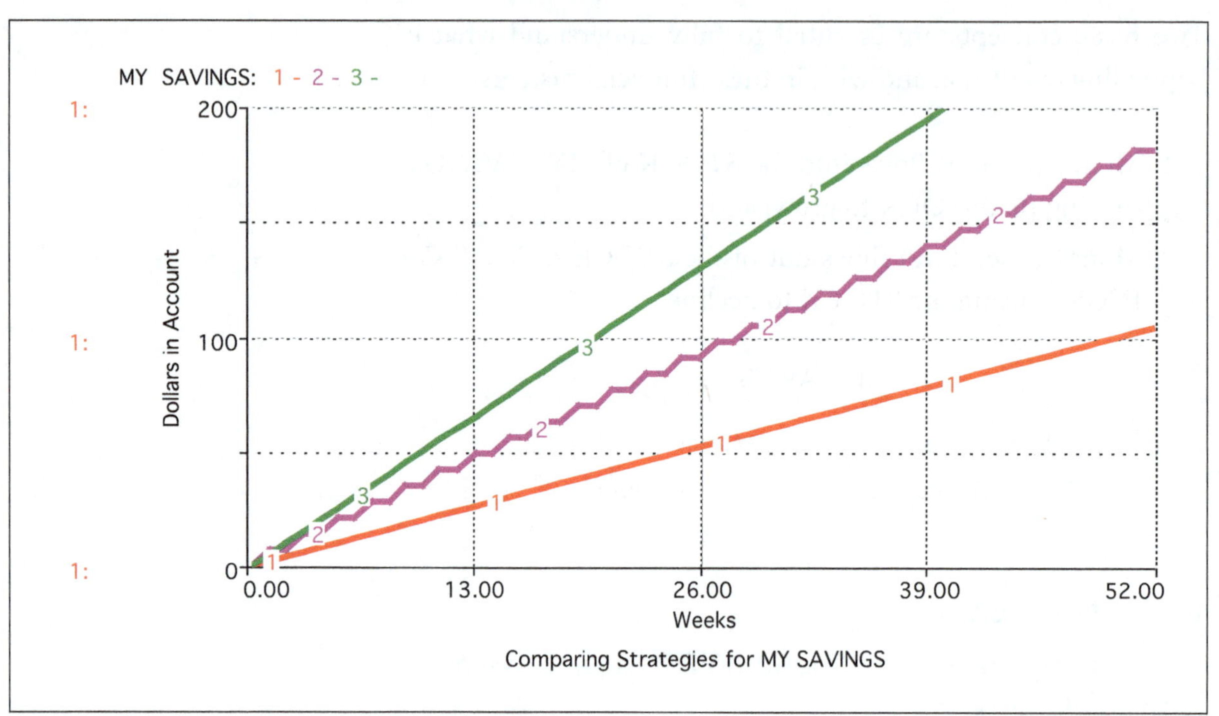

The Graph above illustrates three different Saving PLANS, each designed to reach a $200 GOAL:
(#1) $2 every week, (#2) $10 every 3 weeks, (#3) $5 every week. These are illustrations of three of many options that the students could develop using Worksheet A and the simulation.

B. Spending

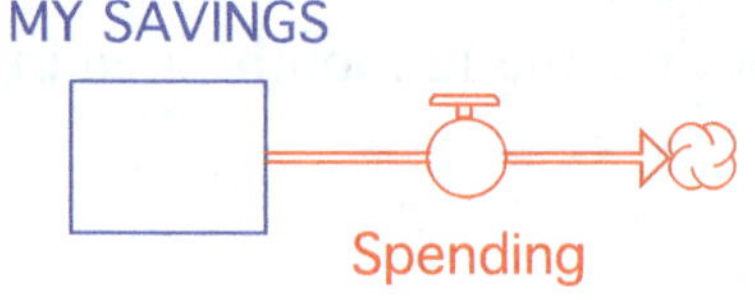

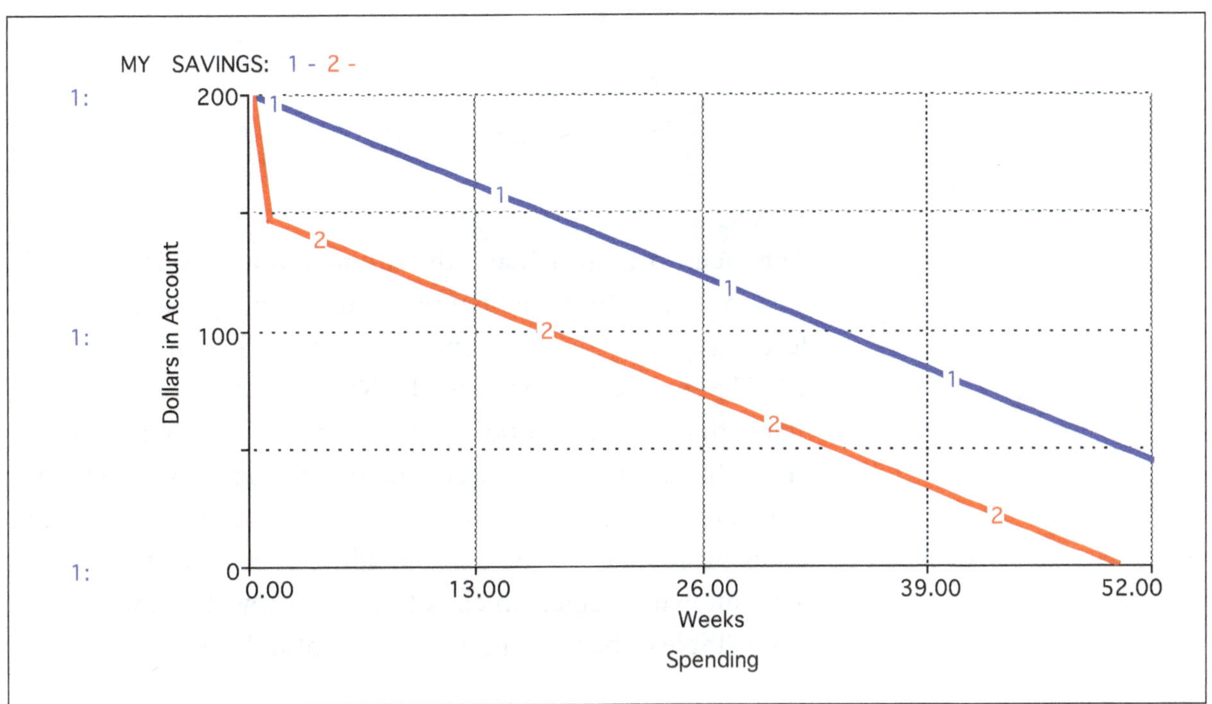

This Graph illustrates different Spending PLANS, each starting with $200. These are two of many examples that the students could develop using Worksheet B and the simulation:
(#1) spend $2 every week; (#2) make $50 large purchase, then spend $2 every week.

> And, where both Spending and Saving are happening at the same time (as in the real world!), the GOAL for successfully managing MY SAVINGS over time is this:
>
> Spend Less Than You Earn.

2. Making a PLAN and Observing Outcomes—The Main Exploration

To engage students, Lesson 2 offers meaningful and open-ended questions for which there are many correct answers. Each student is asked: What is your personal financial GOAL? Can you devise financial PLANS for regular Saving and Spending to achieve that GOAL? Finally, how do you choose your favorite

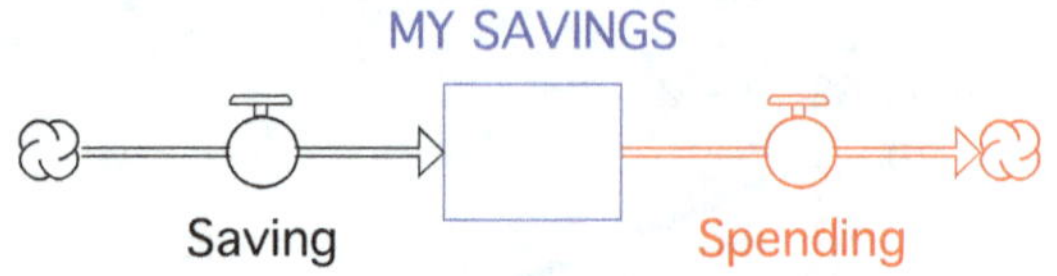

PLAN?

The focus of Lesson 2, and the simulation it uses, is to give the students an open-ended template on which to create their own learning. The lesson assumes students will identify different GOALS and accompanying PLANS. Students need to understand that *communication* is central for evaluating their success. That is, they must be clear in identifying to others (1) their personal GOAL and (2) their choice of financial PLANS that focus on regular Saving and Spending to achieve that GOAL. The following Table, which is filled in below, is presented as a blank Table to be filled in by the student in Worksheet C.

3. Recording at least TWO successful PLANS (or 3, if you like!)

PLAN #	MY SAVINGS GOAL ($)	Weeks Between Deposits	Regular Saving Amount ($)	Cost of Large Single Item ($)	Amount of Regular Weekly Spending ($/wk)	Continue to Save After Reach GOAL? (Y or N)	Final MY SAVINGS ($)
1	500	1	10	200	5	N	30
2	1000	2	25	1000	0	Y	300
3	2000	1	20	1000	25	N	900

4. Using Graphs and Tables

As in Lesson 1, students will use Graphs and Tables to describe and communicate the patterns of change that they observe over time in their accounts (with accounts first growing as SAVINGS accumulate to a GOAL, then falling with Spending). Tables and Graphs can be printed from the simulation or created by the students themselves using Worksheet C. Students will be expected to discuss the distinct strengths of each.

- The Behavior-over-Time Graph is designed to record multiple plans by focusing only on the changing amount of money in the account each week. The example below is

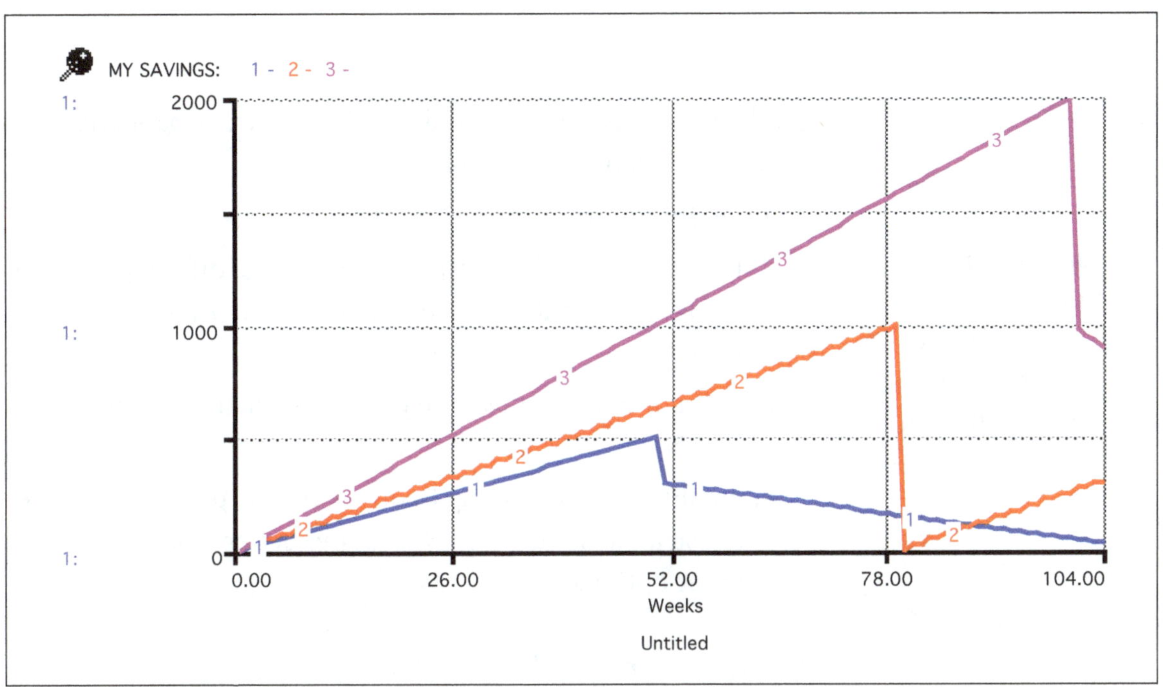

based on the filled Table above.

- The Table below records weekly changes in money saved (inflow), money spent (outflow), and money in MY SAVINGS (the STOCK). Those Flows correspond to the important concepts of financial systems described earlier. This Table shows the final weeks of Plan 3, summarized in the filled Table in section #3.

Weeks	MY SAVINGS	Weekly Saving	Weekly Spending
92	$1,840	$20	$0
93	$1,860	$20	$0
94	$1,880	$20	$0
95	$1,900	$20	$0
96	$1,920	$20	$0
97	$1,940	$20	$0
98	$1,960	$20	$0
99	$1,980	$20	$0
100	$2,000	$0	$1,025
101	$975	$0	$25
102	$950	$0	$25
103	$925	$0	$25
Final	$900		

5. Putting the Pieces Together

Students now ANALYZE and DESCRIBE what happened and why. This involves four steps:

1. Defining their personal GOAL(s);
2. Using a Graph (or Graphs) to compare different options, recognizing that they can devise more than one successful PLAN;
3. Using a Table to describe changes over time of individual PLANS;
4. Finally, communicating to others (peers, parents) why they chose a particular PLAN as being better (for them!) than other options.

A key element of this exercise is developing the idea that there is no single RIGHT answer.

Where and When Will Students Need Guidance?

1. Assuming that students have already completed Lesson 1, they should be familiar with their need (1) to properly record data (record their plans and the consequences) and (2) to understand WHY they got the results that they did. Here it may be appropriate to slow students down, and ask them initially to focus ONLY on their Saving PLAN or ONLY on their Spending PLAN.
2. A key element of this exercise is developing the idea that there is no single RIGHT answer, but that different people can have very different, and quite reasonable, goals and ways to achieve their goals.
3. Since each student will have different GOALS and PLANS, students should understand that they need to provide teachers with a means to follow and evaluate their progress (or problems) with each of those financial elements and their combination into an overall PLAN.
4. The challenge here is in emphasizing the importance of COMMUNICATION as both a tool for testing (Am I happy with these results?) and explaining (Do you understand what I did and why?) plans for Saving and Spending.

Bringing the Lesson Home

? What is the important student-learning from this simulation?

- *Experiencing and solving a problem of the student's own creation.*
- *Understanding and appreciating the importance of math in managing personal finance in order to be successful using different strategies or plans.*
- *Understanding and becoming facile with the utility of Graphs and Tables.*
- *Ability to present what they have learned to others and the ability to learn from the results that others share, through questioning or even (respectfully and constructively) challenging their choices.*

Name____

Saving for a GOAL

Your SAVINGS will grow steadily with regular Saving. **In this exercise, you have a personal SAVINGS GOAL you want to reach in 52 weeks (or less). Use the simulation to explore your options.**

1. Try different PLANS, choosing (a) the amount you will regularly save AND (b) how often you will make a deposit.

2. Record information about your successful PLANS and circle your favorite PLAN.

PLAN 1:

a) GOAL__________

b) Amount of Regular Saving: _____

c) Weeks Between Deposits: _____

d) Weeks to Reach GOAL: ________

PLAN 2:

a) GOAL__________

b) Amount of Regular Saving: _____

c) Weeks Between Deposits: _____

d) Weeks to Reach GOAL: ________

PLAN 3:

a) GOAL__________

b) Amount of Regular Saving: _____

c) Weeks Between Deposits: _____

d) Weeks to Reach GOAL: ________

PLAN 4:

a) GOAL__________

b) Amount of Regular Saving: _____

c) Weeks Between Deposits: _____

d) Weeks to Reach GOAL: ________

3. Using a Table or a Graph (printed from the simulation or hand-drawn), explain which PLAN you prefer and why: ____

____

____

____

Name_______________________________________

Does My Personal Spending PLAN Add Up?

Will the money in MY SAVINGS meet my needs and wants over the next 52 weeks?

How much money was in MY SAVINGS to start? ___________

1. Try different spending PLANS that have (a) a single large purchase, (b) regular weekly purchases, or (c) both.

2. Record information about your successful PLANS here and circle your favorite PLAN:

PLAN 1:

a) Single Large Purchase: $________

b) Regular Weekly Spending: $_____

c) Money Left in Account
After 52 Weeks: $ ________

PLAN 2:

a) Single Large Purchase: $________

b) Regular Weekly Spending: $_____

c) Money Left in Account
After 52 Weeks: $ ________

PLAN 3:

a) Single Large Purchase: $________

b) Regular Weekly Spending: $_____

c) Money Left in Account
After 52 Weeks: $ ________

PLAN 4:

a) Single Large Purchase: $________

b) Regular Weekly Spending: $_____

c) Money Left in Account
After 52 Weeks: $________

3. Using a Table or a Graph (printed from the simulation or hand-drawn), explain which plan you prefer and why: ____

____

____

____

____

Name____

How Can I Reach My Personal Saving and Spending GOAL?

Reaching a financial GOAL means having a Saving and Spending PLAN. Use the simulation provided to test different PLANS to find the one that best satisfies *your* needs or wants.

1. Describe your GOAL (What do you want and when do you want it?).

My personal GOAL is to:____

I want to complete my Saving in ___________ weeks.

2. Use the simulation to test different PLANS of Saving followed by Spending. Record at least TWO successful PLANS (or 3, if you like!) below.

Choices							Results
PLAN #	MY SAVINGS GOAL ($)	Weeks Between Deposits	Regular Saving Amount ($)	Cost of Large Single Item ($)	Amount of Regular Weekly Spending ($/wk)	Continue to Save After Reach GOAL? (Y or N)	Final MY SAVINGS ($)
1							
2							
3							

3. Provide a Graph (printed from the simulation or hand-drawn) showing ALL your successful PLANS; then explain which PLAN you like best and why?

____

____

4. Pick your favorite PLAN and use a Table to answer the following questions:

A. How long did it take you to reach your GOAL for MY SAVINGS? ______ weeks

B. During which weeks were you able to spend money? _______

C. Suggest at least 3 different ways you might have increased the number of weeks you could spend money.

1. ____
2. ____
3. ____

Which of those 3 different approaches do you prefer and why? ____________________

____

____

Lesson 3

Can I Make Money with a Lemonade Stand?

Instructions for Teachers

Student Challenge:

Use a computer simulation to explore the real-world challenges of running a business (a virtual lemonade stand), with the GOAL of maximizing total profit (income minus expenses). Students make important choices (how much lemonade to make and what price to charge per cup) and learn about basic economic principles (price affects sales, purchase volume lowers unit expenses), and how they affect business income, expenses, and profits. In addition, students are encouraged to reflect upon balancing the amount of time spent working (making and selling) and total profits earned.

At the Lesson's End:

- Students will have completed a structured exploration of how Income and Expenses combine to control their ability to achieve a simple business financial GOAL.
- Students will have designed and tested a variety of PLANS for achieving that GOAL.
- Students will have used tables, graphs, and systems thinking concepts to share their results with classmates (and parents!) by doing the following:
  - Comparing successful (and unsuccessful!) PLANS, and
  - Exploring the underlying "values" they brought to this challenge.

(See the following Instructions and the Worksheets for more details.)

NOTE

The material developed in Lesson 1 is strongly recommended to familiarize students with the basic concepts that are used and further ex-panded in this lesson.

MATERIALS

- Computer Simulation (available on-line at http://clexchange.org/curriculum/dollarsandsense/lesson3.asp).
- Two worksheets (use as needed) to record plans and results.

Overview

In Lesson 3 students use a computer simulation to explore the real-world challenges of running a business—in this case, a lemonade stand on a busy street corner on a warm summer's day. Building on the background of Lesson 1, where we introduced the idea of personal savings being controlled by contributions to saving and reductions of spending, students will operate a virtual lemonade stand for five days. Their challenge is to maximize their total profit (income minus expenses). In making and exploring the impact of important choices (how much lemonade to make and what price to charge per cup), they learn about basic economic principles (price affects sales, purchase volume lowers unit expenses), and how these principles affect business income, expenses, and profits.

The simulation's Control Panel, reproduced below, illustrates how choices influence income and expenses and the ultimate profit that results. Line 1 is from a simulation in which 2 batches of lemonade were made each day, with a price per cup set at

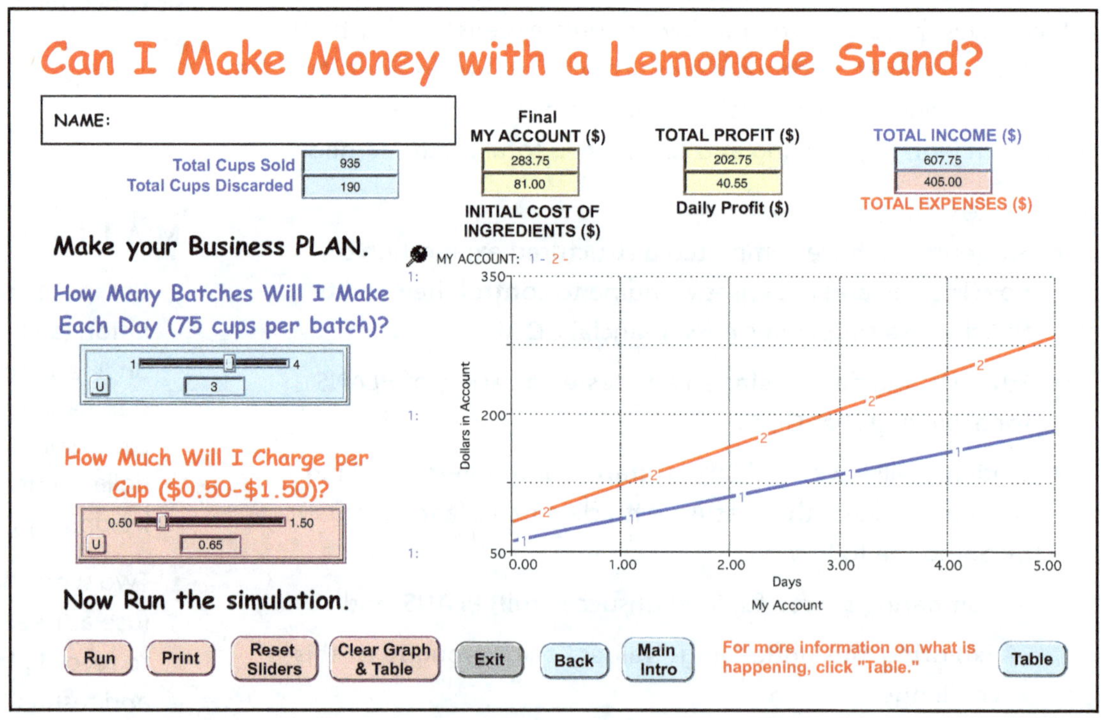

$0.75. Line 2 is from a simulation where 3 batches were made and the price per cup set at $0.65.

Managing a business is similar to managing your personal finances. Your business has a STOCK of money called MY ACCOUNT. Each day that your lemonade stand operates, two things happen: (1) money flows into MY ACCOUNT in the form of Daily Income (based on sales); and (2) money flows out of MY ACCOUNT in the form of Daily Expenses (based on supply costs).

> Where Income and Expenses are both happening at the same time, maximizing one's profits depends on finding ways of boosting Income and/or reducing Expenses.

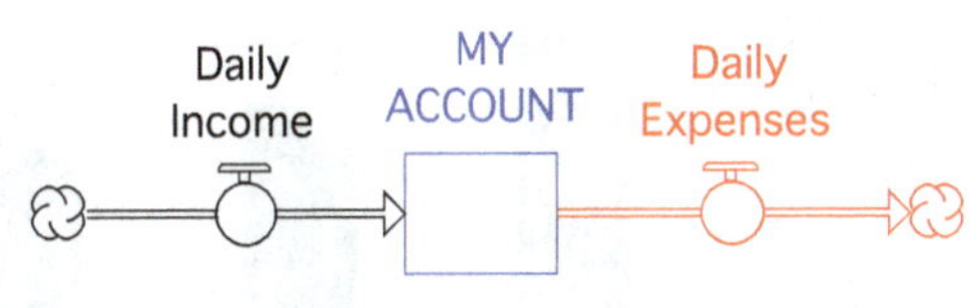

Lesson Structure

1. Understanding the Lemonade Business

Working on paper to develop a conceptual understanding of the system

Running a business requires an understanding of how the system works. In Worksheet A, students are introduced to the basic concepts needed to operate this business profitably.

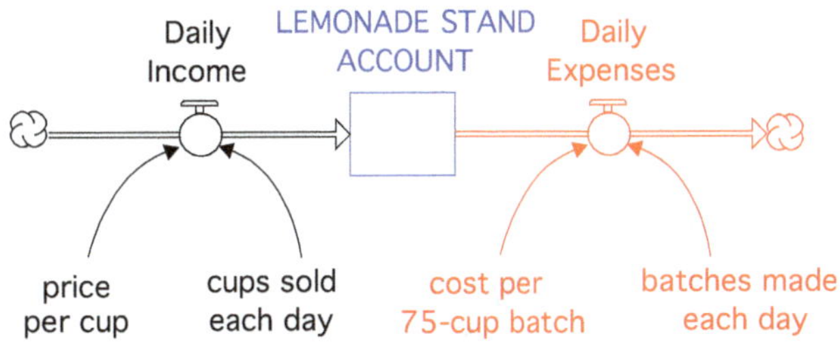

Students are provided with a map that introduces the basic concept of how the Flows of Daily Income and Daily Expenses control how their LEMONADE STAND ACCOUNT changes over time, and the four key factors that affect those Flows. Here, students learn that Income is defined by the price they set per cup and the total number of cups they sell. Expenses are defined by the cost of each "batch" they make (cost of all the raw materials—lemons, sugar, cups, ice, etc.) and the number of batches they make. Two of these (price and batches made) are fully under the control of the students.

Two conceptually challenging real-world factors (Cost per Batch; Cups That Could Be Sold), not fully under the students' control are then graphically presented. Students are then required to interpret two different types of Graphs (a bar Graph for Cost per Batch, and a line Graph for Cups That Could Be Sold).

A. EXPENSES. The more batches of lemonade you make daily, the cheaper will be the ingredients for each batch. (Good questions to ask the students might be "Do you think this is a reasonable assumption?" "Why?")

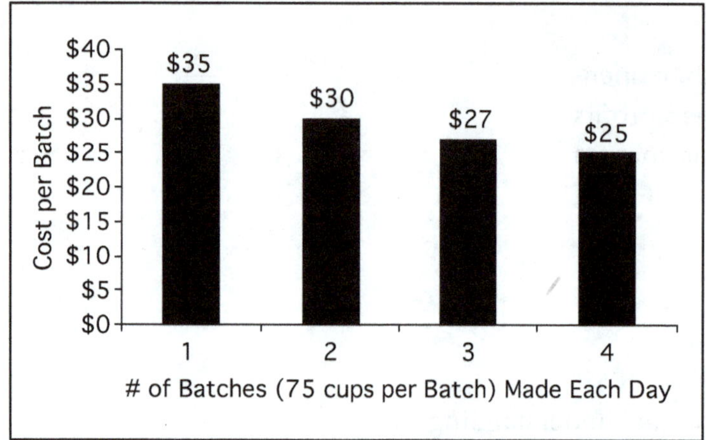

How much will it cost to make the following?

	Per Batch	*Total Cost*
1 Batch	$35	$35
2 Batches	$30	$60
3 Batches	$27	$81
4 Batches	$25	$100

B. INCOME. The number of cups you can sell depends on the price you charge. (Good questions to ask the students might be "Do you think this is a reasonable assumption?" "Why?")

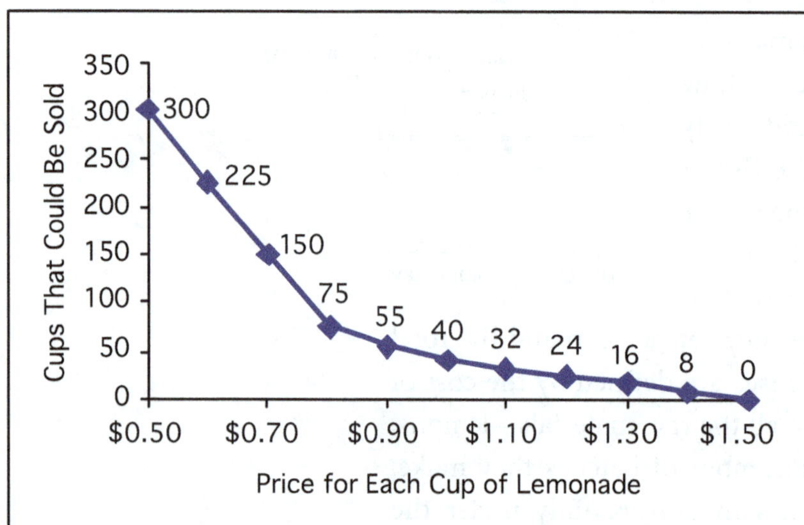

How many cups could you sell, if you charged the following per cup?

Price per Cup	*Cups Sold*
$0.50	300
$0.70	150
$0.90	55
$1.10	32
$1.30	16
$1.50	0

This Graph illustrates a general principle and has been tailored to the conditions defined in the Overview. The number of cups that could be sold at a given price could vary depending on location, on the weather, on the number of advertising flyers posted, etc. The simulation is not crafted to demonstrate those variations, but they could be a fruitful topic of discussion with the students.

Students are also asked to consider an additional variable: "time." For purposes of simplicity, students are instructed that each batch of lemonade requires 2 hours of work to make and sell. Thus, the more batches produced, the longer one works. This variable offers students an opportunity to reflect on trade-offs involving time and profit: more batches may yield more money (total profit), but less "profit per hour worked."

2. Making PLANS and Observing Outcomes

Students now have the conceptual foundation with which to make and test different PLANS.

A. Each student group begins by making two decisions.

- How much will you charge per cup? (any amount between $0.50 and $1.50 per cup)
- How many batches will you make each day? (75 cups per batch; 1 to 4 batches per day)

See lines 1 and 3 in the illustration Table on the following page.

B. Students then use the simulation to see how well their PLAN performs and they record their results. (Illustrative choices are presented below. The same Table is provided as a blank to be filled in as part of Worksheet B.)

	PLAN 1	PLAN 2	PLAN 3	PLAN 4
Price Per Cup ($0.50–$1.50)	$0.50	$0.75	$0.75	$1.25
Cups Sold [each day] (from the simulation Table)	75	75	112	20
Batches Made Each Day (1–4)	1	1	2	1
Cost per Batch	$35.00	$35.00	$30.00	$35.00
MY ACCOUNT (after 5 days)	$47.50	$141.25	$180.00	$25.00 after 1st day no money left to buy materials
TOTAL PROFIT (MY ACCOUNT minus Cost of 1st Day's Ingredients)	$12.50	$106.25	$120.00	-$10.00 (a loss!)
Profit per Hour Worked (simulation Table)	$1.25	$10.63	$6.00	-$5.00 (a loss!)

3. Using Tables and Graphs

As in the previous lessons, students use Graphs and Tables to describe and communicate the patterns of change that they observe over time in their accounts. Tables and Graphs can be printed from the simulation or can be created by the students themselves. Each has distinct strengths that the students should recognize and be prepared to discuss.

- The Behavior-over-Time Graph is designed to record multiple PLANS by focusing only on the changing amount of money in MY ACCOUNT each month. (Four PLANS from the filled Table above are illustrated here.)

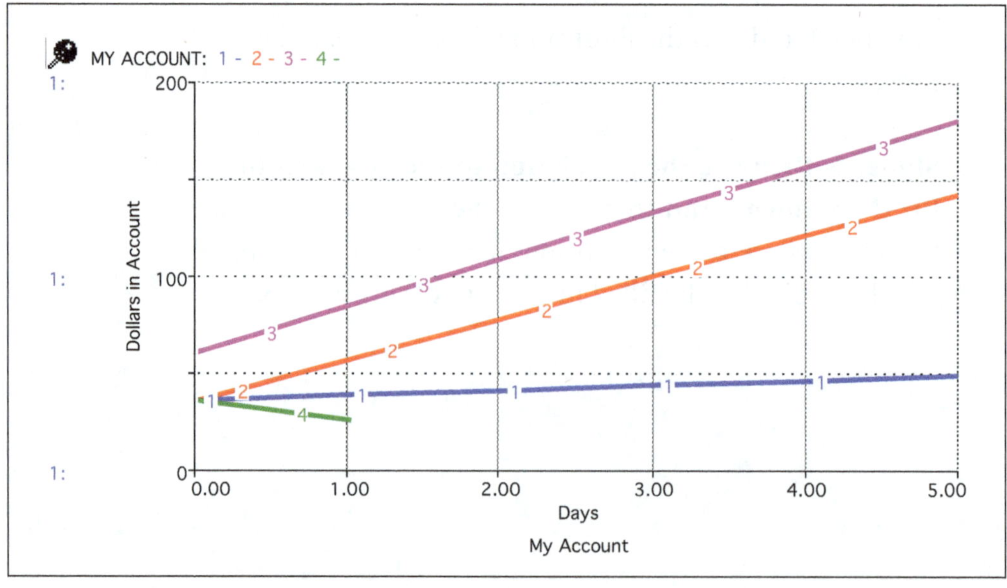

- The Table below illustrates PLAN 2 from the two figures above. The Table records the starting balance of money in MY ACCOUNT each day, Daily Expenses (flowing out of MY ACCOUNT), and Daily Income (flowing into MY ACCOUNT). These Flows define the starting balance of money in MY ACCOUNT on the next day. In addition, the Table records the Lemonade Stand's Daily Profit and both the daily number of cups sold (depending on price, as defined by the bar graph in Section 1) and the daily number unsold (all those made but not sold).

Days	MY ACCOUNT	Daily Expenses	Daily Income	Daily Profit	Cups Sold	Cups Discarded
0	$35.00	$35.00	$56.25	$21.25	75	0
1	$56.25	$35.00	$56.25	$21.25	75	0
2	$77.50	$35.00	$56.25	$21.25	75	0
3	$98.75	$35.00	$56.25	$21.25	75	0
4	$120.00	$35.00	$56.25	$21.25	75	0
Final	$141.25					

4. Putting the Pieces Together

Students now ANALYZE and DESCRIBE what happened and why. Three steps are involved:

1. Using their Graph(s) to compare and evaluate the effectiveness of different options for maximizing profit;
2. Using their Table(s) to explore the details of Income and Expense that generate that profit; and
3. Working with and communicating with each other, to compare the pros and cons of different strategies and to recognize how the pieces of the system work together to produce profits.

Worksheet B is designed to pull these pieces together for the students. In addition to the Table above, Worksheet B challenges the students to be precise in understanding and describing how income and expense are generated. The following illustrates what is requested on Worksheet B, using PLAN #3 from the above Table. Your students' answers for their best PLANS for Daily Income and Expenses might look like this.

Fill in the blanks below.

Daily Income

Describe below, in words, how you calculate Daily Income.

price per cup x *cups sold each day* = *Daily Income*

Calculate Daily Income below using the numbers from your Best PLAN:

$0.75 x 112 = $84.00

Daily Expenses

Describe below, in words, how you calculate Daily Expenses.

cost per 75-cup batch x *batches* = *Daily Expenses*

Calculate Daily Expenses below using the numbers from your Best PLAN:

$30.00 x 2 = $60.00

Where and When Will Students Need Guidance?

1. While this simulation is designed to help students learn by asking better questions, it is critically important that they understand the core economic concepts that underlie how the simulation works. Their business is not a "black box." To appreciate how it generates certain results (how, for instance, high prices lead to low sales), they need to be comfortable with the Basics.

- Help them **see** how price affects sales. (Would I be more likely to buy a small candy bar for $1 or $2?)
- Help them understand the important concept of economies of scale (compare price per ounce of big boxes of cereal versus smaller ones).

2. Interpreting Graphs: We have consciously used two types of Graphs (bar and line) here and have asked students to interpret both. They may not be familiar with both of these graphing styles and may need instruction.
3. Understanding WHYs: Here, it may be appropriate to slow students down, and ask them initially to focus ONLY on their Income strategies or ONLY on their Expenditures. What is the maximum profit possible when making 1 batch? Students could test and evaluate multiple pricing schemes. They could then take that ideal price and see what happens by increasing batches to 2, then 3, then 4. What does this tell them? The worksheets provide teachers with a means to follow and evaluate student progress or problems with each of the financial elements and their combination into an overall PLAN.
4. Computer games focus all too often on "Winning." And while there is a particular set of decisions that will maximize profit, we want students to appreciate that there are different levels of "success." One can, for instance, make a profit without working all day as you must when making 3 or 4 batches. We provide a calculation of 'profit per hour' to help students see that, while profits from multiple batches may be higher, those higher profits come with diminishing returns as the students need to work for more hours than they may prefer. Comparing PLANS allows students to recognize a range of options that may have particular virtues beyond the particular GOAL of 'highest profit.'

We want students to appreciate that there are different levels of "success."

Bringing the Lesson Home

? What is the important student-learning from this simulation?

- *Interpreting Graphs: Students are challenged to work with bar and line Graphs (showing relationships between two variables, e.g., cost per batch and number of batches made, or price per cup and number of cups sold) as well as another kind of line Graph, the Behavior-over-Time Graphs produced by the simulation. Recognizing how to work with each Graph, and recognizing the value of different Graphs, comprises an important element of learning here.*
- *Understanding and appreciating the importance of math in running a business; being successful exploring different strategies or PLANS; and understanding the utility of Graphs and Tables.*
- *Gaining the means and opportunity to apply learning beyond this particular illustration: Though the simulation does have two "best" answers (there is one particular strategy which yields the greatest total profit here, another that generates greatest profit per hour worked), it is equally important that the student recognize the limits of this simulation by framing "better questions"; e.g., What if there's competition? Hot, or cool and rainy weather? Franchising? Learning may be most powerful when students think outside the box.*
- *Learning about opportunities to create their own business problem. Seeing and applying what they have learned to a personal scenario is, of course, the most meaningful of all options.*

Extending the Learning

We touched on some possible areas for exploration and discussion above.

? What is the relationship of price per cup and amount of lemonade that can be sold?

How might that Graph (and your business PLAN) change during a hot spell? During a cool, drizzly period?

? What sort of profit per batch (or per unit of time) do the various strategies produce?

The maximum business profit requires making and selling 3 batches (225 cups) of lemonade each day. If you assume that making and selling three batches will take three times as long as a single batch, could a $30 profit for 2 hours of work be better than a $50 profit for 6 hours?

? Is there a way to combine the benefit of buying in quantity with the relatively higher profits per hour for smaller quantities?

Could you recruit some additional friends to set up separate stands a couple blocks apart and share the savings for buying 3 batches of ingredients each day?

Name_______________________________________

Can I Make Money With a Lemonade Stand?

Understanding Your Business

You and your best friend decide to open a lemonade stand in your neighborhood and run it for 5 days. Your GOAL is to make as much PROFIT as you can in those 5 days. Sounds simple, but...The computer simulation will help you explore options.

You will need to make two DECISIONS.

- How many batches (75 cups per batch) will you make each day? Bear in mind the following.
  - Unsold lemonade will be thrown away at the end of each day.
  - The more batches you make, the longer it will take to sell them.
- How much will you charge per cup of lemonade (price per cup)?

1. In the "real world," how do you make a PROFIT?

Recognize that money will be moving in and out of your account each day. Your PROFIT is the difference between how much comes in (Income) and how much goes out (Expenses). PROFIT = Income – Expenses.

Your Daily Income and Daily Expenses are affected by four factors.

A. Two decisions you make:

Factor 1: the price you set per cup; and

Factor 2: the number of batches you make each day.

AND

B. Two additional factors that depend on those first decisions:

Factor 3: the cost per batch (enough ingredients to make 75 cups); and

Factor 4: the number of cups sold each day.

In the figure at right, draw lines connecting the Daily Income and the two factors that control it. Connect to the Daily Expenses the two factors that control them.

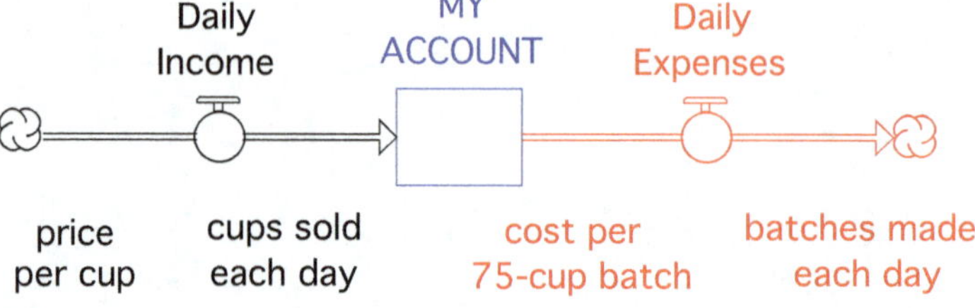

Name____

Examine the Graphs below to understand how Factors #3 and #4 work.

Factor #3: Cost per Batch: The more batches of lemonade you make each day, the cheaper will be the ingredients for each batch, because you are buying more.

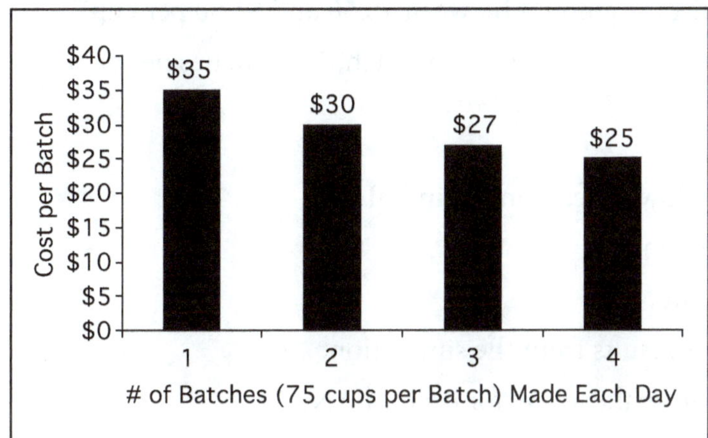

How much will it cost to make lemonade?

	Cost Per Batch	*Total Cost*
1 Batch	______	______
2 Batches	______	______
3 Batches	______	______
4 Batches	______	______

Factor #4: Cups Sold Each Day: The number of cups you sell depends on the price you charge.

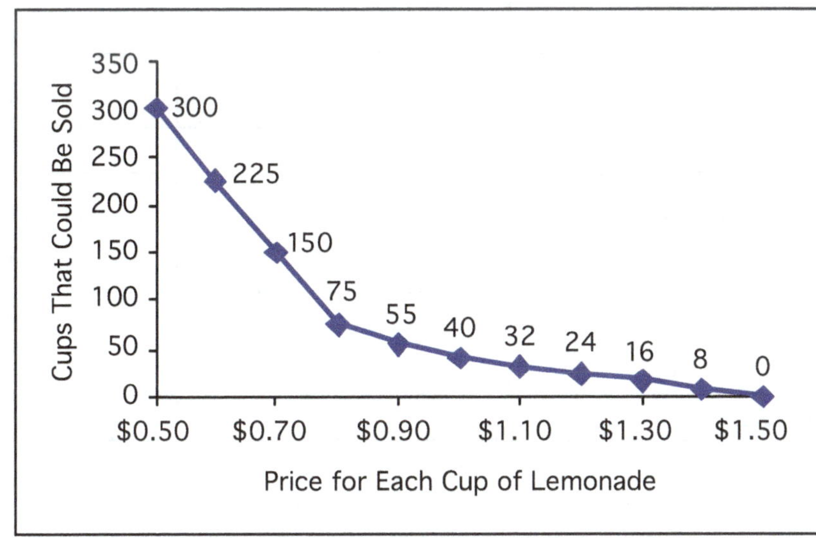

How many cups will you sell, if you charge the following price per cup?

Price Per Cup	*Cups Sold*
$0.50	______
$0.70	______
$0.90	______
$1.10	______
$1.30	______
$1.50	______

Name____

Can I Make Money With a Lemonade Stand?
Using the Simulation

1. It is time now to make and test a PLAN. You will need to decide the following.
- How much will you charge per cup? (any amount between $0.50 and $1.50 per cup)
- How many batches will you make each day? (75 cups per batch; 1–4 batches per day)

Then, do the following.
- Record those choices in the Table below (lines 1 and 3, **in bold**).
- Enter those decisions into the simulation.
- Run the simulation to see how you did.
- Fill in the rest of the Table with your results from the simulation.

Experiment with different PLANS, repeating the above for each PLAN.

And don't forget, your GOAL is to make as much PROFIT as possible.

	PLAN 1	PLAN 2	PLAN 3	PLAN 4
Price Per Cup ($0.50–$1.50)				
Cups Sold [each day] (from the simulation Table)				
Batches Made Each Day (1–4)				
Cost per Batch				
MY ACCOUNT (after 5 days)				
TOTAL PROFIT (MY ACCOUNT minus Cost of 1st Day's Ingredients)				
Profit per Hour Worked (simulation Table)				

Circle the number of the PLAN in which you made the greatest profit (your BEST PLAN).

2. Use the figure below to help calculate your BEST PLAN's Daily Income and Daily Expenses.

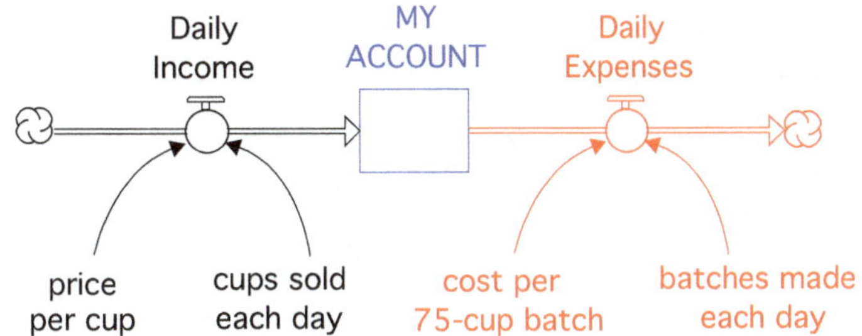

Fill in the blanks below.

Daily Income:

Describe below, in words, how you calculate Daily Income.

________________ x ________________ = ________________

Calculate Daily Income below using the numbers from your BEST PLAN.

________________ x ________________ = ________________

Daily Expenses:

Describe below, in words, how you calculate Daily Expenses.

________________ x ________________ = ________________

Calculate Daily Expenses below using the numbers from your BEST PLAN.

________________ x ________________ = ________________

How does this information explain why you made the greatest PROFIT with a particular set of decisions (price per cup and number of batches made)? ________________________

____

You can calculate your PROFIT per hour worked (daily profit divided by hours worked per day). When you think about PROFIT that way, do any of your PLANS look better? Why?

____

____

Do you think this is how other businesses work? WHY or WHY NOT? ________________

____

____

Lesson 4

Can I Successfully Run the Local Food Bank?

Instructions for Teachers

Student Challenge:

Use a computer simulation to explore options for "successfully" running a local Food Bank for 10 weeks. "Success" involves balancing weekly food donations with weekly demands for food while trying to maximize the "good" the food donations can do (defined in terms of the number of families being assisted and the amount of food distributed to each family). In learning the basics of how non-profit organizations such as Food Banks operate, students learn to think about different strategies for sustaining these efforts.

At the Lesson's End:

- Students will have completed a structured exploration of managing the financial health of a Food Bank by learning to balance food donations (the inflow of food) with food assistance (the outflow of food) to those in need.
- Students will have designed and tested a variety of PLANS for achieving dual objectives of sustaining the Food Bank and maximizing the good it does for the community.
- Students will have used tables, graphs, and systems thinking concepts to share their results with classmates (and parents!) by doing the following:
  - Comparing successful (and unsuccessful!) PLANS, and
  - Exploring the underlying "values" they brought to this challenge.

(See the following Instructions and the Worksheet for more details.)

NOTE

The material developed in Lesson 1 is strongly recommended to familiarize students with the basic concepts that are used and further ex-panded in this lesson.

MATERIALS

- Computer Simulation (available on-line at http://clexchange.org/curriculum/dollarsandsense/lesson4.asp).
- Worksheet to record plans and results.

Overview

In Lesson 4 students use a computer simulation to explore options for managing a non-profit organization. As in the case of a personal account, managing a non-profit Food Bank involves balancing inflows and outflows, but the Flows consist of food (Donation and Distribution) rather than money (Saving and Spending). A second and perhaps more significant difference exists between managing a non-profit (such as a Food Bank) and managing personal finances. In personal finance, the GOAL is to maximize inflow to the STOCK (MY ACCOUNT). In a non-profit Food Bank, the GOAL is to maximize (sustainably!) the outflow (Food Distributed Weekly) from the STOCK (TOTAL FOOD IN FOOD BANK) to maximize the good the Food Bank can do. The opportunity for students to use this lesson to explore this real-world challenge adds powerful hands-on learning in the following ways:

- Recognizing and challenging preconceptions;
- Explicitly identifying choices; and
- Evaluating outcomes.

The simulation's Control Panel, reproduced below, provides an illustration of how these learning elements are developed as students explore and tailor a variety of PLANS. The illustration compares two PLANS that differ only in the "Pounds of Food per Family Each Week": PLAN #1 is set at 30 "Pounds of Food per Family Each Week," and PLAN #2 is set at 25 "Pounds of Food per Family Each Week."

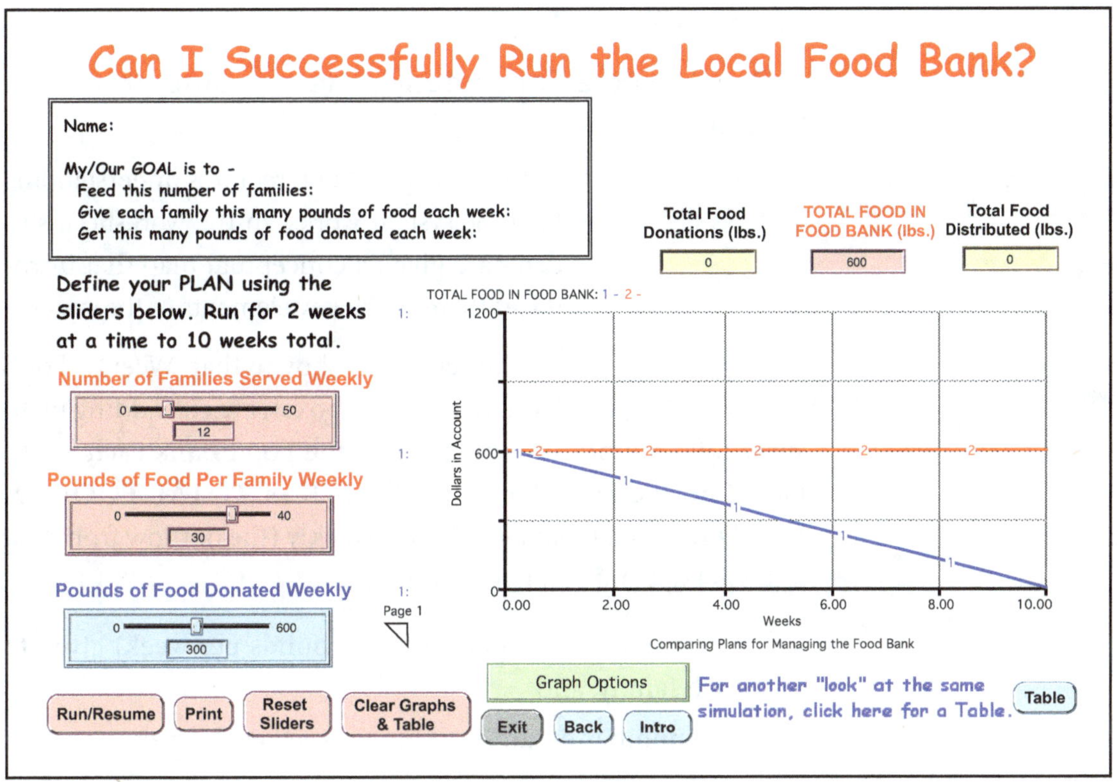

To more fully understand what is happening over time and why, the students' management PLANS reflect a conceptual system, in which the following takes place.

1. Weekly Food Donations flow into the STOCK of TOTAL FOOD IN FOOD BANK, causing that STOCK to grow; and
2. Food Distributed Weekly flows out of the STOCK of TOTAL FOOD IN FOOD BANK, causing the STOCK to decline.

The GOAL of a Food Bank is to maximize the outflow of food (Food Distributed Weekly) to those in need. Unlike the STOCK of SAVINGS, the GOAL is NOT to maximize the STOCK of TOTAL FOOD IN FOOD BANK.

Lesson Structure

1. Developing a Conceptual Understanding of the "System"

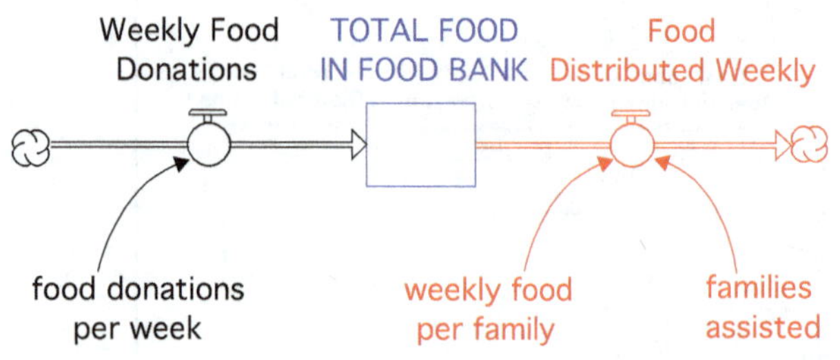

Running a Food Bank requires understanding how the system works. In the worksheet, students are given a conceptual map that introduces them to the key elements of the system.

Students are shown that Weekly Food Donations (cans, boxes, etc., all adding up to some total pounds of food given to the Food Bank each week) Flow into the Food Bank (the STOCK of **TOTAL FOOD IN FOOD BANK**). Food Distributed Weekly (the outflow from that STOCK) depends on two factors:

1. The amount of food (again, in pounds per week) given to each family, and
2. The number of families being served each week.

2. Making Plans and Observing Outcomes—The Main Exploration

A second challenge is to wrestle with a particular scenario—specifically to be responsible for running the Food Bank for a 10-week period. In this simulation, students learn the following:

- The local Food Bank starts with 600 pounds of food on its shelves.
- 12 families have been getting food from the Food Bank each week.
- Each family gets 30 pounds of food per week.
- Donations of food have averaged 300 pounds per week.

A. What will happen, if current patterns continue?

Students will use the simulation to answer that question. As shown below, the Table presented in the simulation shows that the Food Bank will have run out of food by the end of their ten-week management! Similar insights can be achieved with the Graph provided by the simulation.

Week #	TOTAL FOOD IN FOOD BANK	Food Distributed Weekly	Weekly Food Donations
0	600	360	300
1	540	360	300
2	480	360	300
3	420	360	300
4	360	360	300
5	300	360	300
6	240	360	300
7	180	360	300
8	120	360	300
9	60	360	300
Final	0	----	----

B. **A second option is then presented:** Families served increase from 12 to 15 each week. This reveals an even greater problem, as shown in the Graph produced by the computer simulation. The more dramatic fall of the red line (#2 for the second situation) signals that the Food Bank would run out of food even faster—in a mere 4 weeks. Similar insights can be achieved with the Table provided by the simulation.

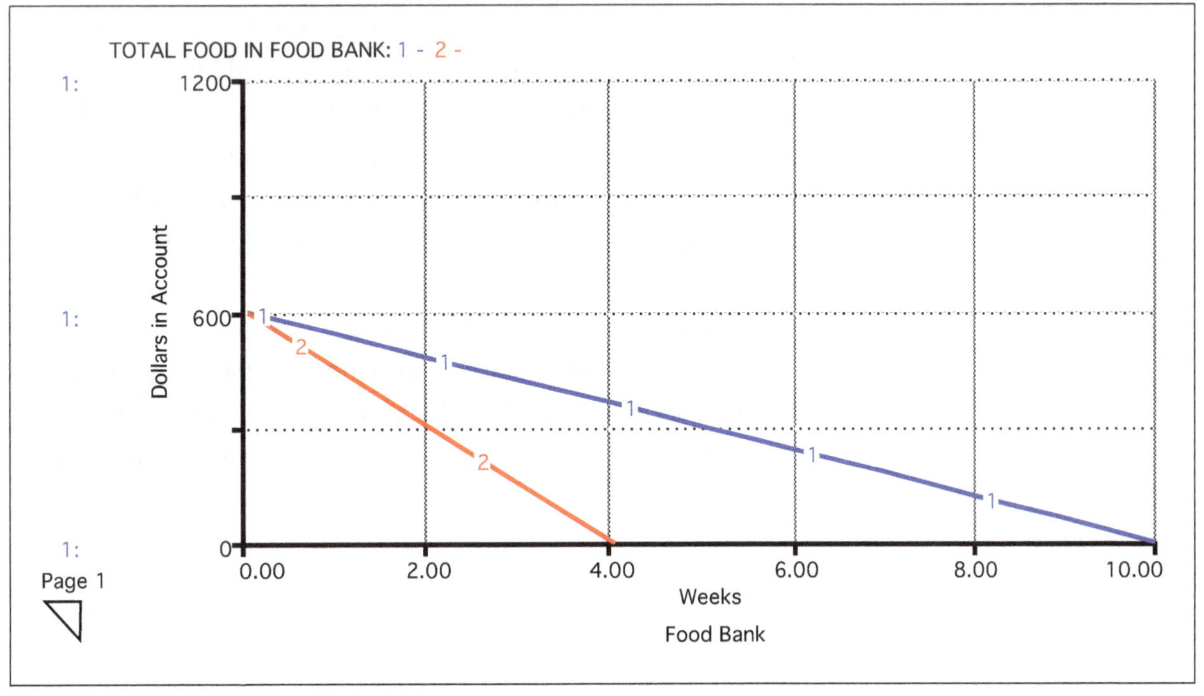

C. **Making Alternative Plan(s) and Observing Outcomes**
Having thus recognized the problem, students are asked a simple question: **What can you do about it?**

Using the simulation to explore different PLANS, the challenge is to manage the Food Bank's inflow (donations) and outflow (distribution to families) of food in a responsible and sustainable manner. **The GOAL is to do the most good possible while keeping the Food Bank in operation.** Running out of food means the Food Bank will have to close down.

Students will use the simulation to explore different PLANS and to record their results. Four PLANS (of many possible options) are illustrated below.

	PLAN 1	PLAN 2	PLAN 3	PLAN 4
Food Donated (Pounds per week)	300	300	350	400
Number of Families Served	12	10	12	12
Food Distributed per Family (Pounds per week)	30	30	25	30
TOTAL FOOD IN FOOD BANK at end of 10 weeks (Pounds)	0	600	1100	1000

3. Using Tables and Graphs

Students will work with Tables and Graphs to describe and communicate the patterns of change that they observe over time in the Food Bank. Tables and Graphs can be printed from the simulation or created by the students themselves using the last page of the worksheet. Each has distinct strengths that the students should recognize and be prepared to discuss.

- The Behavior-over-Time Graph is designed to record multiple PLANS by focusing only on the changing amount of TOTAL FOOD IN FOOD BANK each week (illustrated here with the four PLANS recorded above; colors correspond).

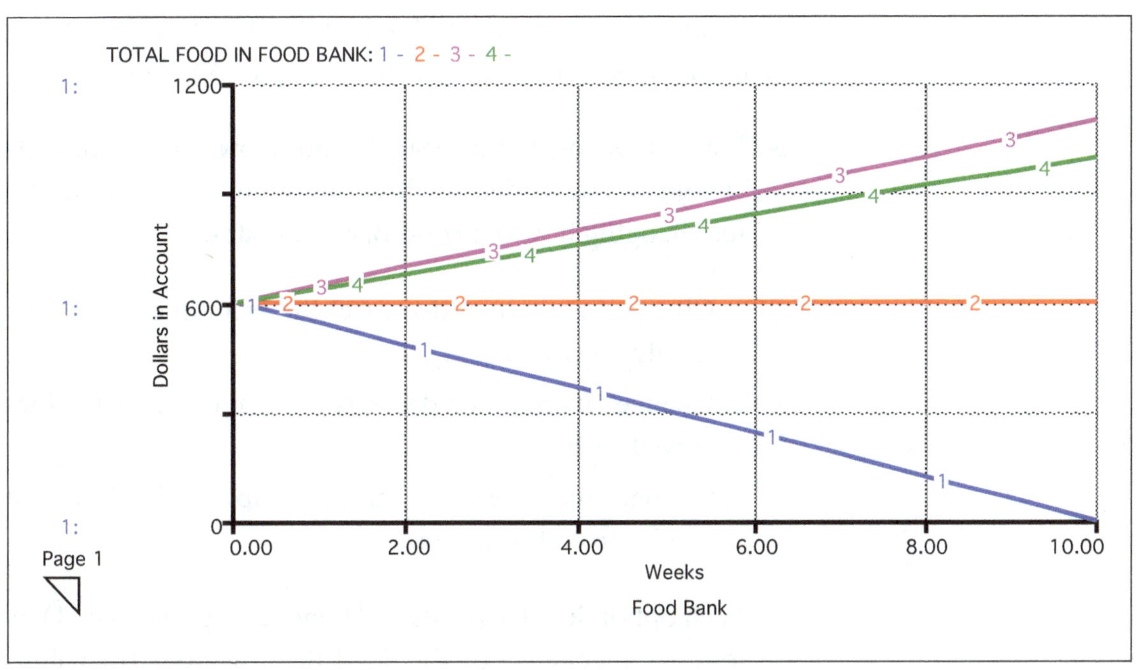

- The Table records TOTAL FOOD IN FOOD BANK (starting with 600 pounds), Food Distributed Weekly (outflow), and Weekly Food Donations (inflow) *for a single PLAN*. Illustrated below is PLAN #4.

Week #	TOTAL FOOD IN FOOD BANK	Food Distributed Weekly	Weekly Food Donations
0	600	360	400
1	640	360	400
2	680	360	400
3	720	360	400
4	760	360	400
5	800	360	400
6	840	360	400
7	880	360	400
8	920	360	400
9	960	360	400
Final	1,000		

4. Putting the Pieces Together

Students are responsible for ANALYZING and DESCRIBING what happened and why; for evaluating and discussing several different PLANS they explored to keep the Food Bank running sustainably; and, finally, for explaining which PLAN they like best.

A. Using the conceptual (Stock and Flow) map, students should be able to identify three options or "leverage points" for changing how the Food Bank operates.

   1. Change (increase or decrease) the amount of food each family receives weekly.
   2. Change (increase or decrease) the number of families served each week.
   3. Change (increase!) the amount of food donations you receive from the community.

B. Each option involves costs and benefits experienced (1) by food recipients; (2) by the Food Bank workers (or volunteers) who are responsible for soliciting the food; or (3) by the larger community asked to support the Food Bank.

C. Students should be able to use their Graph(s) to compare and evaluate the effectiveness of different options for sustaining the Food Bank and maximizing the good it does.

D. Students should be able to use their Table(s) to evaluate how weekly contributions and weekly distributions together define the changing TOTAL FOOD IN FOOD BANK.

E. Finally, working with and communicating with others, students should be able to compare observations and to recognize how the pieces of the puzzle work together. In that process, they discover there are a number of ways to sustain the system, each with its own set of costs and benefits. But there is no single right answer.

Where and When Will Students Need Guidance?

1. This simulation is designed to help students learn to ask better questions as they think about how to maximize the good they can do in managing a Food Bank (or any non-profit). The following concepts can encourage such questioning:

A. Understanding the three different options or "leverage points" for managing the Food Bank.

B. Recognizing "costs" and "benefits" of those different options that would be borne (1) by food recipients; (2) by the Food Bank workers (or volunteers) who are responsible for soliciting the food; or (3) by the larger community asked to support the Food Bank.

2. Many schools are engaged with local social service providers such as Food Banks. Connecting this exercise to such ongoing or potential real-world activities is likely to strengthen learning from both.

Connecting this exercise with local service projects students are doing can strengthen learning from both.

3. The structure of the Tables produced by the STELLA software may need some explanation. The best way to read the Tables is to recognize that the TOTAL FOOD IN FOOD BANK values for each week represent the *ending* value for that week. So, the Table above at Week 4, can be read as: at *the end of Week 4* we have 760 pounds in the Food Bank. We then (during week 5) distribute 360 pounds and take in 400 pounds, so that at *the end of Week 5* (the start of the next row) we have 800 pounds in the Food Bank, a net increase of 40 pounds during the 5th week.

4. Interpreting Graphs: The Graphs that we present to the students in this simulation provide students with two ways to look at these dynamics. On Page 1 of the Graph Pad, they can compare the overall impacts of several different PLANS. Page 2 of the Graph Pad presents both the STOCK and the two Flows for a given PLAN.

5. Understanding WHYs: Here, it may be appropriate to slow students down, and ask them initially to focus ONLY on food donation strategies or ONLY on food distribution. The worksheets provide teachers with a means to follow and evaluate student progress or problems with each of these elements and their combination into an overall PLAN.

Bringing the Lesson Home

? What is the important student-learning from this simulation?

- *Interpreting and working with Tables and Graphs: Students work with and learn from Tables and Behavior-over-Time Graphs. Recognizing how to work with each, in addition to recognizing the value of each, comprises an important element of learning here.*
- *Understanding and appreciating the importance of math skills in running a non-profit such as a food bank.*
- *Being successful in exploring different strategies or PLANS.*

Extending the Learning

Expanding the application of the simulation beyond this specific illustration: This simulation offers a template for students to use in considering a variety of non-profit operations. They can use the knowledge gleaned in this exercise to ask how other non-profit entities strive to maximize the good they do while wrestling with real-world challenges.

Name____

Can I Successfully Run the Local Food Bank?

Student Challenge: You are being given the responsibility to manage the Food Bank within your community for the next 10 weeks. Can you do it? The computer simulation will help you test your PLANS and explore options.

Here is what you need to know about your challenge.

- At the moment, the Food Bank has 600 pounds of food on its shelves.
- On average, 12 families have been getting food from the Food Bank each week.
- Typically, each family gets 30 pounds of food per week.
- During the past several weeks, donations of food have averaged 300 pounds per week. However, weekly donations previously averaged 350–400 pounds, so donations have decreased.

1. Start by understanding how a Food Bank works in the "real world." The Food Bank's Director identifies three factors (food donations, food given to each family, and number of families assisted) that control what is happening each week, as they take in donated food and give it out again to needy families.

In the figure below, connect to the inflow VALVE the factor (or factors) that control the amount of the Weekly Food Donations (the inflow); then connect to the outflow VALVE the factor(s) that control the amount of Food Distributed Weekly (the outflow).

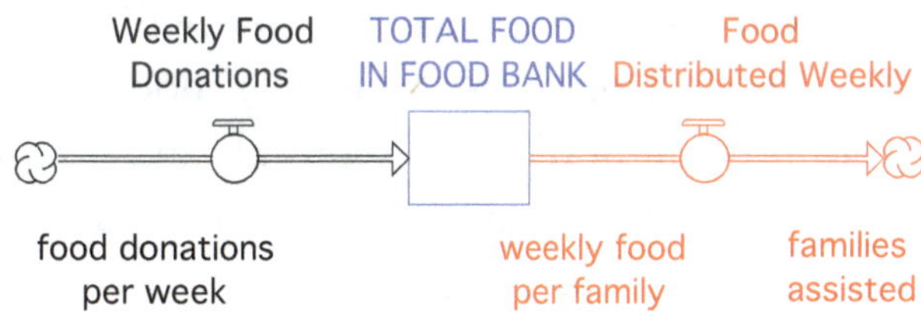

Use that information to explain (in words) the definitions of the following.

A. Weekly Food Donations =

____

B. Food Distributed Weekly =

____

C. TOTAL FOOD IN FOOD BANK =

____

Name____

Can I Successfully Run the Local Food Bank?
Using the Simulation

1. Making PLANS. Remember, the Food Bank currently has 600 pounds of food on its shelves. The Manager advises you of TWO possible situations (described below) that may arise over the next 10 weeks. Use the simulation to explore what will happen to the amount of FOOD IN FOOD BANK over the next 10 weeks in each situation.

SITUATION 1:	What Will Happen to the Food Bank? Describe below.
Weekly Food Donations (300 pounds of food donated per week to the Food Bank) and Food Distributed Weekly (30 pounds per family each week to 12 families) remain the same.	

SITUATION 2:	What Will Happen to the Food Bank? Describe below.
Weekly Food Donations remain the same for the next 10 weeks, BUT the number of families receiving food increases from 12 to 15.	

2. Now, use the simulation to explore different ways to deal with these situations. Remember, your challenge is to manage the Food Bank's donations (inflow) and its distribution of food to families (outflow) in a responsible and *sustainable** manner. Keep track of your PLANS and their results on the table below so that you can explain to your classmates, parents, or teacher what you tried and how it worked.

Your GOAL is to do the* most good possible *while keeping the Food Bank in operation. If you run out of food, you will have to close down. Keep in mind that each action that you take will have costs and benefits for someone in your community. Keeping costs and benefits in mind is part of your planning process.

	PLAN 1	PLAN 2	PLAN 3	PLAN 4
Food Donated (Pounds per week)	300	300	350	400
Number of Families Served	12	10	12	12
Food Distributed per Family (Pounds per week)	30	30	25	30
TOTAL FOOD IN FOOD BANK at end of 10 weeks (Pounds)	0	600	1100	1000

* "Sustainable" means the Food Bank will keep a continuous supply of food on its shelves to allow it to keep operating.

Name____

3. Which of these PLANS do you like best? ______ Explain why below.

____

____

____

4. Analyze your results.

A. What 3 different actions could make the Food Bank sustainable? (Hint: You may want to refer to the Stock and Flow Map at right to remind yourself how the "system" works!)

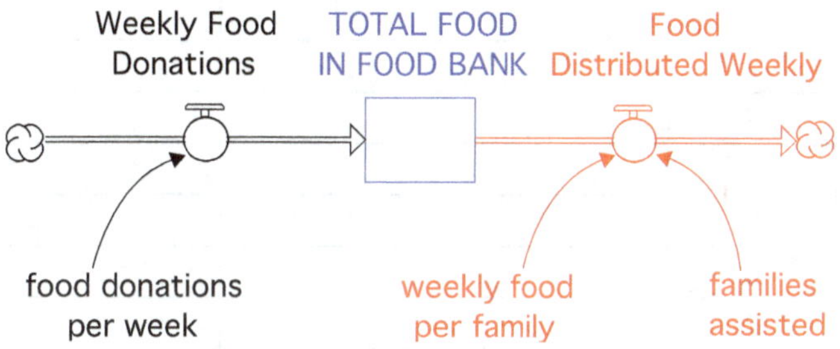

1. ____

2. ____

3. ____

B. Which of these actions did you use in the PLAN you liked best? ______________

C. Prepare a Graph and a Table (next page or print from the simulation) that shows your favorite PLAN. You will use these in Step 5 where you discuss and compare PLANS with others.

D. Each action has costs and benefits to different people in your community. For the PLAN you like best, indicate the following:

1. What are the benefits and who will receive them? ______________________

____

2. What are the costs and who will pay them? __________________________

____

5. Be prepared to discuss your favored PLAN and its results (costs and benefits) with your teacher and your classmates.

Name_______________________________________

Favorite PLAN

- Weekly Food Donations: ___________
- Number of Families Assisted: ___________
- Weekly Food Per Family: ___________

Week #	TOTAL FOOD IN FOOD BANK	Food Distributed Weekly	Weekly Food Donations
0	600		
1			
2			
3			
4			
5			
6			
7			
8			
9			
Final			

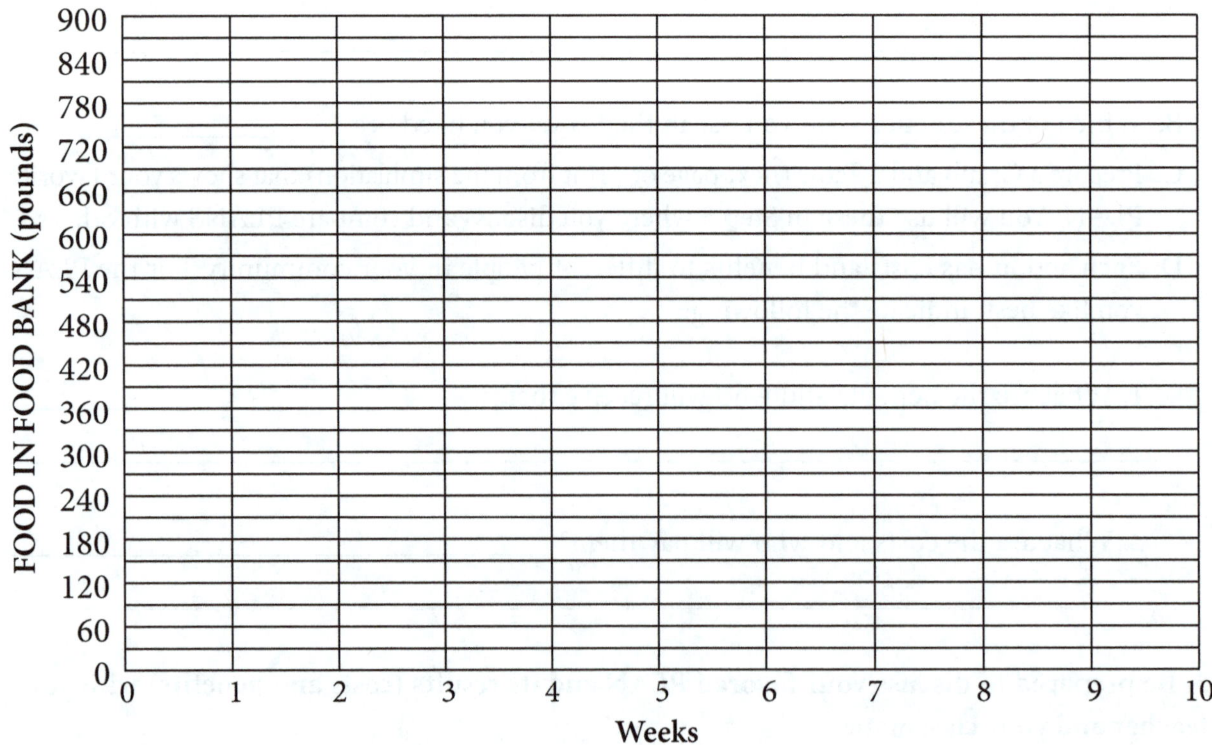

Lesson 5

Can I Help a Responsible Teen Buy a Car?

Instructions for Teachers

Student Challenge:

Use a computer simulation to help a friend buy a first car by exploring the real-world challenges of balancing work responsibilities with other time demands (schoolwork and fun), and income with expenses, in pursuing that savings GOAL.

- Students will have completed a structured exploration of how Income and Expenses combine to control their ability to achieve a challenging financial GOAL.
- Students will have designed and tested a variety of PLANS for achieving that GOAL.
- Students will have used tables, graphs, and systems thinking concepts to share their results with classmates (and parents!) by doing the following:
  - Comparing successful (and unsuccessful!) PLANS, and
  - Exploring the underlying personal "values" they brought to this challenge.

(See the following Instructions and the Worksheet for more details.)

NOTE

The material developed in Lesson 1 is strongly recommended to familiarize students with the basic concepts that are used and further ex-panded in this lesson.

MATERIALS

- Computer Simulation (available on-line at http://clexchange.org/curriculum/dollarsandsense/lesson5.asp).
- Worksheet to record plans and results.

Overview

The GOAL of purchasing a car, much like any other personal finance GOAL, involves DEVISING and TESTING a PLAN with two elements: Saving and Spending. In this simulation, students are provided a hands-on opportunity to explore options for earning money (summer and/or school-year jobs) and spending money, each involving "trade-offs" such as giving up time and/or spending in the short term for a longer-term GOAL of having a car. The simulation's Control Panel, reproduced below, illustrates how these learning elements are developed as students explore and tailor a variety of PLANS. PLAN #1 shows the teen working 40 hours per week only in the summer; PLAN #2 shows the teen working 20 hours per week in the summer and 10 hours per week during the school year. In both PLANS Weekly Expenses are $50. NOTE that **neither** achieves the $5000 goal in 2 years/104 weeks!

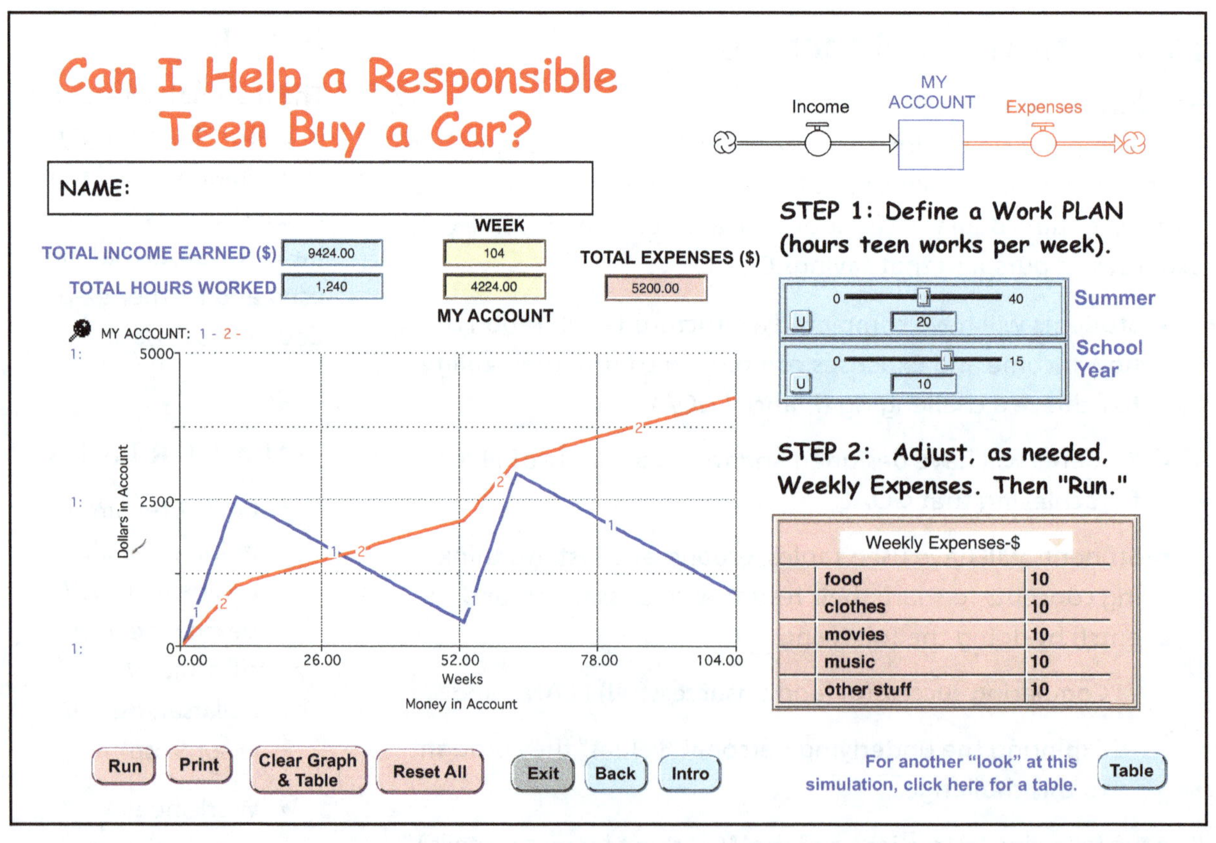

This lesson uses the conceptual structure developed earlier in Lesson 1.

- Money (Income, generated by working) flows into the STOCK, MY ACCOUNT, causing the stock to increase; and
- Money (Expenses) flows out of MY ACCOUNT, causing the STOCK to decline.

Remember: to save a large sum of money, the key remains:

Spend Less Than You Earn.

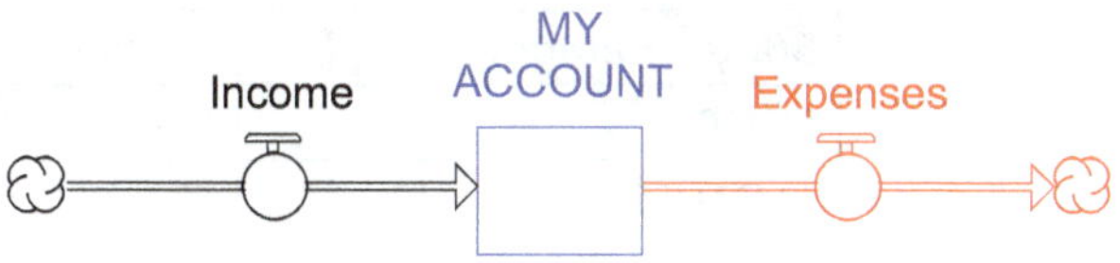

Income
MY ACCOUNT
Expenses

Lesson Structure

1. Working on Paper to Develop a Budget Plan

This exercise focuses on growing one's savings (much as in Lesson 1). The added real-world challenge here is to help a friend make budget decisions that involve two important trade-offs: income versus free time, and short- versus long-term spending. The central focus of Lesson 5 continues to be the accompanying simulation, but here that simulation provides a means to test students' PLANS and implications of the choices they are called on to make.

A. The first decisions focus on **Income** (the inflow of money into MY ACCOUNT). Time must be available for work, potentially sacrificing time for fun or studies. What is a reasonable balance? Currently, the teen works 20 hours a week during the 10 weeks of summer (earning minimum wage, or $6.70 per hour after taxes). Students must make the following decisions: How many hours will you recommend that your teenager work during the summer and, perhaps, during the school year? And do you foresee any potential problems or issues with this PLAN when you and your teen present it to a parent?

B. The next decisions involve **Expenses**. Regular weekly spending means that the MY ACCOUNT will take longer to fill to its $5000 target. Is your teenager willing to balance (give up or reduce) short-term "wants" against larger long-term goals? And what is a reasonable balance?

This simulation begins with the assumption that the teenager has expenses of $50 per week spread among five adjustable categories (see Table below). The choice students make here is—Should the current expenses be changed?

Budget Category	Current Weekly Expenses	Your Choice
FOOD	$10 (e.g., sodas, 1 fast food meal)	
CLOTHES	$10 (for something small; or save for several weeks for something more expensive).	
MOVIES	$10 (1 a week)	
MUSIC	$10 (downloads; or CD)	
OTHER	$10 (changes from week to week)	
TOTAL WEEKLY EXPENSES:	$50	

2. Making a PLAN and Observing Outcomes—The Main Exploration

This lesson, and the simulation at its core, is primarily focused on giving students an open-ended challenge to test a variety of PLANS (with their accompanying trade-offs) over a 2-year (104-week) period to save $5000 to buy a car.

3. Recording at least THREE successful PLANS (more if you like!)

Students are challenged to devise and explore several PLANS. Three, of the **many** possible PLANS, are illustrated in the Table below.

	Choices				Results
PLAN #	Summer Work (Hours per Week)	School Year Work (Hours per Week)	Total Weekly Expenses ($ per Week)	Does the PLAN Succeed? (Yes or No)	If Successful, How Long Did It Take (In Weeks)?
1	40	0	50	No	—
2	20	10	50	No	—
3	40	10	50	Yes	58 weeks

4. Using Graphs and Tables

Students will work with Graphs and Tables to describe and communicate the patterns of change that they observe over time in their accounts (MY ACCOUNT). These Graphs and Tables can be printed from the simulation or created by the students themselves. Each has distinctive strengths.

- The Behavior-over-Time Graph allows students to compare different PLANS. Illustrated below are the 3 PLANS defined earlier in the Table above; colors match that Table. Note that only PLAN 3 (working 40 hours a week in the summer and 10 each week during the year, while continuing to spend $50 each week) is successful, at least of the three PLANS illustrated.

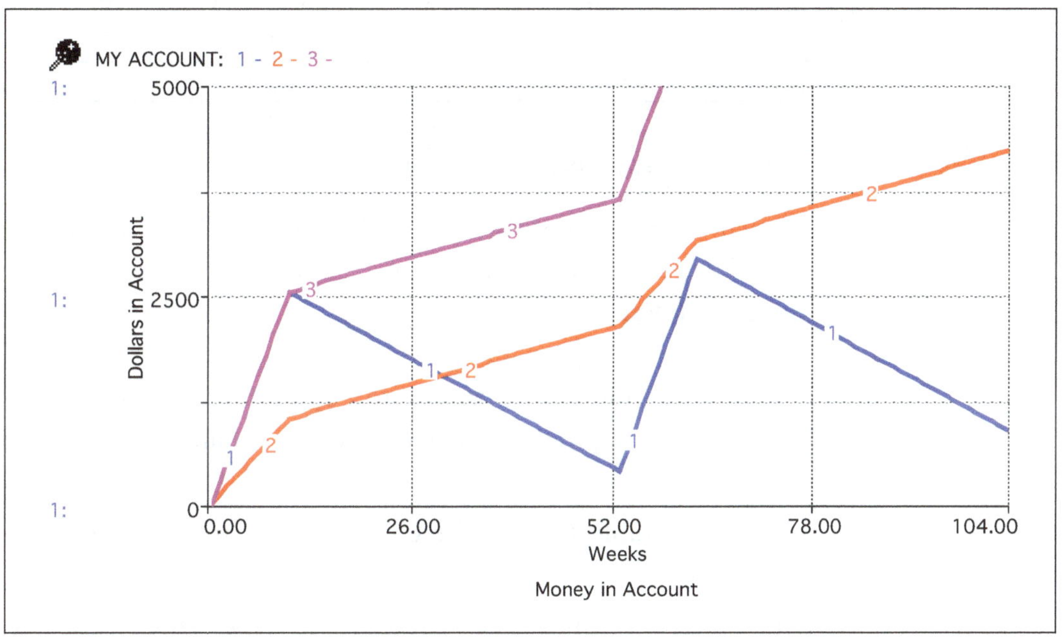

- The Table records changing amounts of savings in MY ACCOUNT as a result of weekly additions of income (generated by summer and school-year work) and subtractions based on regular weekly expenses. The partial Table shown below illustrates the earliest weeks of PLAN 1 in which the teen doubles the prior level of summer work (from 20 to 40 hours per week) but does not work during the school year. Note that expenses remain constant. Recall that in this case, the $5000 GOAL is not reached in two years (104 weeks).

Weeks	MY ACCOUNT	Expenses	Income	Hours Worked
0	$0.00	$50.00	$304.00	40
1	$254.00	$50.00	$304.00	40
2	$508.00	$50.00	$304.00	40
3	$762.00	$50.00	$304.00	40
4	$1,016.00	$50.00	$304.00	40
5	$1,270.00	$50.00	$304.00	40
6	$1,524.00	$50.00	$304.00	40
7	$1,778.00	$50.00	$304.00	40
8	$2,032.00	$50.00	$304.00	40
9	$2,286.00	$50.00	$304.00	40
10	$2,540.00	$50.00	$0.00	0
11	$2,490.00	$50.00	$0.00	0
12	$2,440.00	$50.00	$0.00	0

5. Putting the Pieces Together

Students are responsible for ANALYZING and DESCRIBING what happened and why. As part of that process, they need to do the following:

A. Use a Graph (or Graphs) to compare different options, recognizing that they can devise more than one successful PLAN.

B. Use a Table to describe changes over time of individual PLANS.

C. Finally, communicate with others why they chose a particular PLAN as being better (for them) than other options.

Where and When Will Students Need Guidance?

1. Assuming that students have already completed Lesson 1, they should be familiar with their need to (1) properly Record Data (record their PLANS and the consequences) and (2) understand WHY they got the results that they did. Here, it may be appropriate to slow students down, and ask them initially to focus ONLY on their Saving PLAN or ONLY on their Spending PLAN.

2. The core challenge here is to move students beyond finding the "Winning" answer. There are many successful ones. ***This simulation encourages students both to explore options and to evaluate important trade-offs.*** Students need to explicitly consider: What is my teen willing to "give up" or sacrifice (on income and/or expense sides of the system) in order to save enough for a car?
3. Understanding WHYs: Because this exercise explicitly incorporates "time" as a limited resource (to be used for fun, for study, or for work), it is important that students slow down and think how a parent might respond to a particular plan. Should a teen work year-round? Should a teen work 40 hours a week in the summer? How should a teenager's time be allotted? All work? All play? All study? Or some combination of each?

Bringing the Lesson Home

? What is the important student-learning from this simulation?

- *Understanding and appreciating the importance of math in the following situations:*

  a. Planning for a large purchase;

  b. Exploring, successfully, different strategies or plans; and

  c. Understanding the utility of Graphs and Tables.

- *Understanding how to compare, discuss, and even (respectfully and constructively) to disagree on their choices. Learning will be powerful where and when students learn from one another.*

Extending the Learning

- This simulation provides a template for students to think about personal finance as a multi-faceted endeavor, involving trade-offs that need to be incorporated into their PLAN(S). Ideally, saving for a large purchase will inspire questions about other large purchases: both how to accumulate the needed funds and what needs to be sacrificed in the short term to receive long-term benefits.

Students can be challenged to distinguish between "needs" and "wants."

- Students might also be challenged here to distinguish between "needs" and "wants." Needs are traditionally defined as the basic necessities of life: shelter, food, basic clothing, and healthcare. Wants are desired, but not essential for life.
  - Under what circumstances might a car be a "need" (e.g., to earn income for necessities)? A want?
  - How do the weekly expenses fit along the "need to want" spectrum? How do weekly expenses compare in importance to the car? How does one balance between such "needs" and "wants"?
- Although it is beyond the scope of this lesson, another way to make a large purchase is to borrow the money for it and then repay the loan over some period of time (**paying** interest rather than earning it!) while you make immediate use of the purchase. The idea of borrowing, which is fundamental to financial literacy and the subject of an anticipated future Module, could be a fruitful topic of conversation between students and teachers.

Name____

Can I Help a Responsible Teen Buy a Car?

You have agreed to help a teenager create a PLAN to save $5000, needed to buy a safe car, pay for insurance, and thus win parental approval. Remember, this PLAN, which may take up to 2 years (104 weeks) to achieve, needs to be acceptable to both teenager and parents! **A computer simulation will help you explore options.**

1. Before using the simulation, you will want to develop a BUDGET (a PLAN) for Income and Expenses.

A. INCOME

Currently the teenager works 20 hours each of the 10 weeks of summer vacation (earning $6.70 an hour, after taxes). ***How many hours will you recommend that your teenager work?*** Don't forget, you have to "sell" this PLAN to the teen's parent!

During the School Year: ____________ During the Summer: ____________

B. EXPENSES

This simulation assumes that the teenager has TOTAL WEEKLY EXPENSES of $50 per week (see below). Should that be changed? How? Specify below.

Budget Category	Current Weekly Expenses	Your Choice
FOOD	$10 (e.g., sodas, 1 fast food meal)	
CLOTHES	$10 (something small; or save for several weeks for something more expensive).	
MOVIES	$10 (1 a week)	
MUSIC	$10 (downloads; or CDs)	
OTHER	$10 (changes from week to week)	
TOTAL WEEKLY EXPENSES:	$50	

2. Use the simulation to test different PLANS and record results in the table below.

	Choices				Results
PLAN #	Summer Work (Hours per Week)	School Year Work (Hours per Week)	Total Weekly Expenses ($ per Week)	Does the PLAN Succeed? (Yes or No)	If Successful, How Long Does it Take to Reach $5,000 (Weeks)?
1					
2					
3					
4					

Name____

3. Graph 3 successful plans on 1 graph (printed from the simulation or created on your own), and then explain the following.

A. What do the 3 PLANS have in common?

____

____

B. What is different about each of the 3 PLANS?

____

____

4. Next, select your favorite PLAN to be presented to the parents. Use a table to do the following.

A. Identify 3 "sacrifices" or trade-offs, involving money and time, your teenager will have to make with this PLAN.

1. ____
2. ____
3. ____

B. What do expect your teen's parents to ask after hearing this PLAN? And how should the teenager be prepared to respond?

Parents' Question(s)/Concern(s):

____

____

Teenager's "Best" Response(s):

____

____

5. Be prepared to discuss the following.

A. What have you learned about saving for a big purchase (like a car), in terms of both MONEY and TIME?

B. What do we mean by making trade-offs to make big purchases? What did your teen have to give up in order to achieve that GOAL?

Lesson 6

How Does Interest Grow My Savings?

Instructions for Teachers

Student Challenge:

Lesson 6 recognizes that the mathematics of compound interest is likely to be a challenge for some students. To help them understand the concept, students are given two exercises.

- In Exercise 1, students work with pencil and paper to explore how the compounding process works in the "real world", using 5-day illustrations of the spread of rumors, of disease, and of an offer to double the money in an account each day.
- In Exercise 2, students use a computer simulation to explore the impact of different rates of compounding interest over different periods of time in a savings account.

In both exercises, the GOALS are (1) to introduce students to the powerful (and often explosive) nature of compound growth, as it plays out over time, and (2) to offer a real-world understanding of the potential power of compound interest (which Albert Einstein reputedly called "the most powerful force in the universe!") in shaping their personal finances.

At the Lesson's End:

- Students will have completed a structured exploration of how the process of compounding growth, which involves what systems thinkers call a reinforcing feedback system, affects not only their personal finances, but also a number of other social and biological systems.
- Students will have used tables, graphs, and systems thinking concepts to explore the impact of different interest rates and periods of time on their personal finances, and they will be able to share their results with classmates (and parents!) in comparing different strategies.

(See the following Instructions and the Worksheets for more details.)

NOTE

The material developed in Lesson 1 is strongly recommended to familiarize students with the basic concepts that are used and further ex-panded in this lesson.

MATERIALS

- Computer Simulation (available on-line at http://clexchange.org/curriculum/dollarsandsense/lesson6.asp).
- Two worksheets (use as needed) to record PLANS and results.

Overview

This lesson contains two separate exercises. First, students learn about the general process of compounding as it influences not only personal finance, but also other processes such as the spread of rumors and the spread of disease. Common to all of these is a systems concept called "reinforcing feedback."

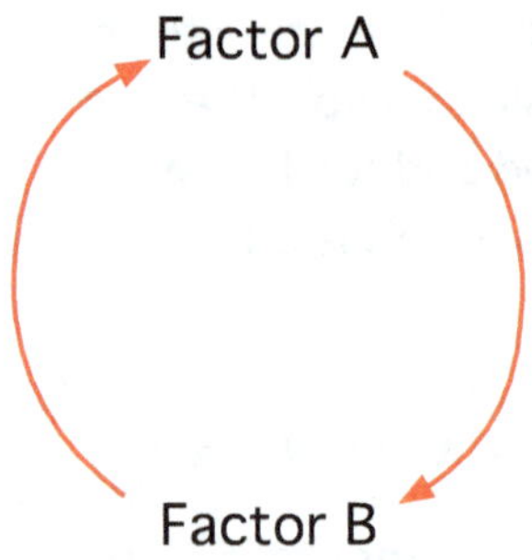

Reinforcing feedback is a type of circular causality, where a change in one factor causes a change in another factor (or factors) in the same direction and then cycles back to cause the original factor to change again in the original direction (see loop). Often described as generating "virtuous" or "vicious" cycles, reinforcing feedback leads either to increasing growth or decline over time.

Second, is an exercise that utilizes a computer simulation and focuses explicitly on compound interest in a bank savings account. The simulation's Control Panel, reproduced below,

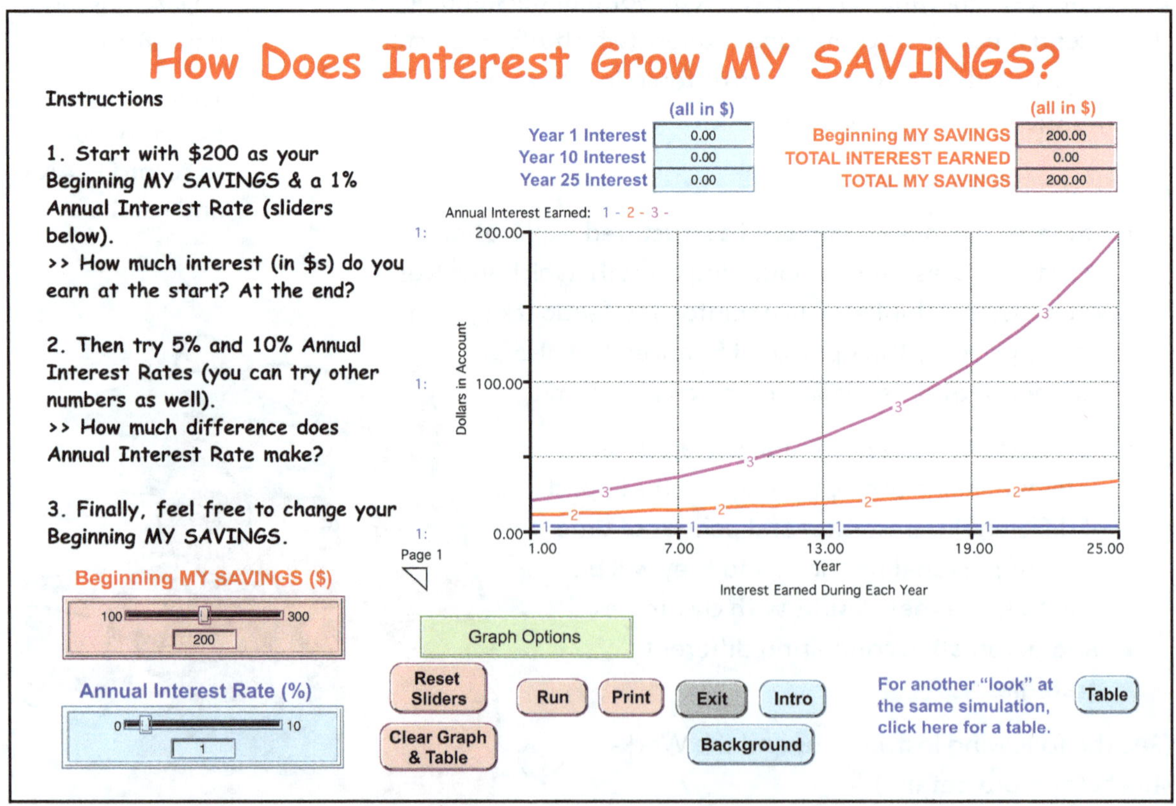

illustrates the impact of different interest rates (1%, 5%, and 10% respectively for PLANS 1, 2, and 3) on an initial savings account of $200 over a 25-year period).

Students will observe that the amount of Interest Income they receive each year grows at an ever-increasing rate (NOT a constant interest being earned each year or even a linearly increasing interest!). That is because the amount of Interest Income the bank pays each year is governed by two factors:

a. The amount of money in MY ACCOUNT; and
b. An interest rate paid by the bank.

Each year's Interest Income is added to MY ACCOUNT, so that the base for next year's interest payment will include interest paid in previous years.

Compound interest is an example of reinforcing feedback. Interest income added to MY ACCOUNT increases the amount of money in that STOCK of money. The next time interest is calculated, there is additional interest because now there is more money in MY ACCOUNT. This happens each time, resulting in still more money in MY ACCOUNT . . . and so on.

If left alone for a long period of time,
the reinforcing feedback produces explosive growth.

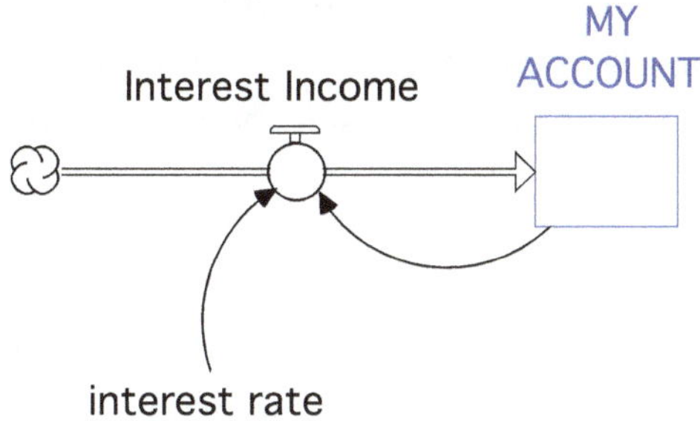

Lesson Structure

Two separate exercises are contained in this lesson: the first looks at the process of compounding from a broad conceptual perspective, and the second uses a simulation to explore the dynamics of compound interest.

Exercise 1. How Does Compounding Work?

Working on Paper to Develop a Conceptual Understanding of the System

1. Developing a Basic Understanding of the Compounding Process

The process of compounding growth is a common part of our lives. Students will select (or be assigned) one of three "everyday" illustrations and then do the following: (1) calculate (using a Table and Graph) how compounding leads to ever accelerating growth and (2) use a Stock and Flow Conceptual Map and Causal Loop Diagram to better represent how the compounding process works. The three illustrations are described below.

- **Rumors:** 1 person starts a rumor. Each day for 5 days, that person tells 1 other, each of whom, in turn, tells 1 other each day, each of whom tells 1 other each day, … and so on. How many people (rumor mongers) are spreading the rumor after 5 days?
- **Infection:** A person becomes sick and remains sick for 5 days. Each day, that person infects 2 others; they each infect 2 others each day, each of whom infects 2 each day, … and so on. How many sick people are there after 5 days?

A powerful hands-on lesson, "The Infection Game," contained in Creative Learning Exchange's *The Shape of Change* curricula, offers students the opportunity to physically simulate the spread of an infection in a classroom and graph the results. For more information, see www.clexchange.org.

- **An Offer You Can't Refuse:** Your father offers you a choice; he will (1) give you $100 today, or (2) give you $1, and then each day for the next 5, he promises to add 2 dollars for every 1 you already have. How much will you have after 5 days with that second offer?

2. Using Graphs and Tables

As in the previous lessons, students use Graphs and Tables to describe and communicate the patterns of change that they observe over time in the three illustrations. Each has distinct strengths that the students should recognize and be prepared to discuss.

- The Graph provides a powerful visual representation of the compounding process (non-linear growth).
- The Table records the size of the STOCK daily **and** the rate of change (the inflow).

Illustration 1:

Graph

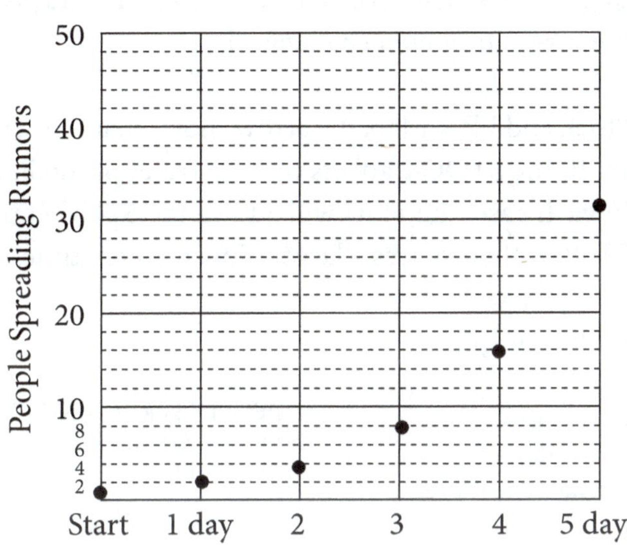

Table

Days	STOCK	Daily Change
0	1	1
1	2	2
2	4	4
3	8	8
4	16	16
Final	32	----

Illustration 2 or 3:

Graph

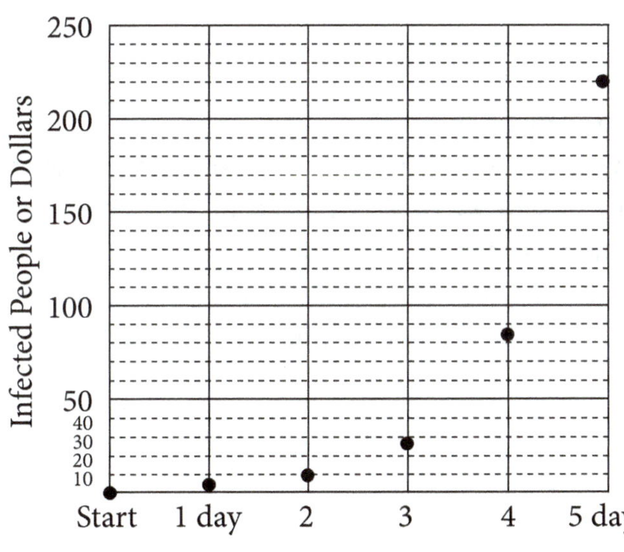

Table

Days	STOCK	Daily Change
0	1	2
1	3	6
2	9	18
3	27	54
4	81	162
Final	243	----

3. Telling a Story using Conceptual Systems Thinking Tools

Students use two systems thinking tools—Stock and Flow Maps and Casual Loop Diagrams—to diagram and describe the common dynamics of compounding. These tools contain important causal arrows that explain what is happening in the system and why.

Using both a Stock and Flow Map and Casual Loop Diagram, each of the three stories is illustrated below (with answers given for each of the three numbered challenges).

- In the Stock and Flow Map, the arrow shows that the accumulation in the STOCK affects the size (rate) of the Flow. Thus, in each case, the Flow will add to the STOCK; that larger STOCK then causes a larger Flow the next time.

Stock and Flow Map

FLOWS:
1. New Rumormongers
2. People Become Ill
3. New Dollars added to my Account

STOCKS:
1. PEOPLE SPREADING RUMORS
2. SICK PEOPLE
3. MY DOLLARS

Flow:____________ **STOCK:**____________

Causal Loop Diagram

- In the Causal Loop Diagram, the first arrow shows that one element causes a change in a second; the second arrow shows that this change in turn causes a change in the original element in the same (or reinforcing) direction. An "R" inside the loop indicates a Reinforcing Feedback Loop.

1. New Rumormongers
2. People Become Ill
3. New Dollars added to My Account

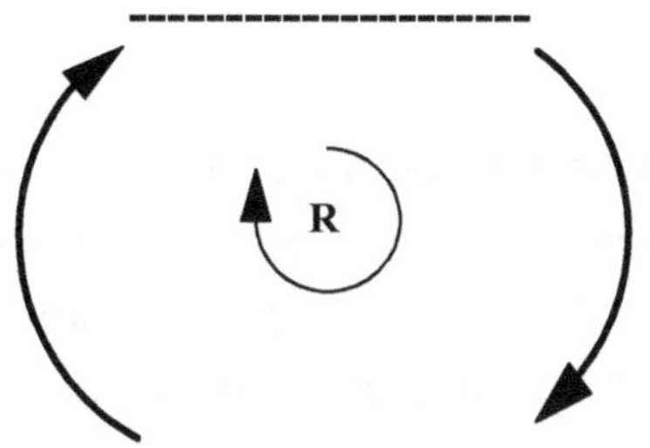

1. PEOPLE SPREADING RUMORS
2. SICK PEOPLE
3. MY DOLLARS

Some people prefer telling stories with Stock and Flow Maps; others use Causal Loop Diagrams.

4. Putting the Pieces Together (Exercise 1)

Students now ANALYZE and DESCRIBE the common story in all three illustrations.

A. Each of the three illustrations involves a compounding or Reinforcing Feedback Loop, where the STOCK affects the size of the Flow (and *vice versa*). As the STOCK grows, the Flow increases, which then increases the STOCK, which increases the Flow still more … and so on, leading to compound or exponential growth. Hence, the stories about the three illustrations are similar.

   1. One rumormonger tells a second on day 1, making a total of 2 rumormongers at the end of day 1; on day 2 those 2 tell 2 more (making 4); on the next day the 4 tell 4 more … and so it goes.
   2. A single infected person infects 2 more people on day 1, making a total of 3 infected people at the end of day 1; each of the resulting 3 infects 2 more people on day 2 (adding 6 more for a total of 9) … and so on.
   3. A single dollar generates 2 more on day 1 making a total of $3 at the end of day 1; each of those $3 generates 2 more on day 2 (adding $6 more for a total of $9) … etc.

B. Students see a Reinforcing Feedback Loop operating in a variety of other familiar contexts, such as the following examples:

1. Spreading rumors or infections could easily be converted to word-of-mouth advice: "I bought one of these, so should you." We can see that phenomenon in "fads"—the right clothing to buy, the best new electronic device to buy, the newest hairstyle, etc.
2. The world of finance is built on growth: "Good" companies are those that report that their sales are growing (over last quarter or year); if a company is able to double its sales each year—wow!
3. Noise in the lunch room can also show reinforcing growth. As people talk, the NOISE LEVEL (a STOCK) increases. That means people have to talk louder to be heard ('making more noise' is the Flow), causing the NOISE LEVEL to increase further, ... and so on, to bedlam.
4. On a less obvious front, emotions or behaviors often are subject to reinforcing growth; for instance, anger builds on itself (we talk about it festering). On a more positive side, a little confidence can also lead to more confidence, and so on.

Exercise 2: Earning Interest on a Savings Account

An Introduction to Compounding Interest - Simulation

In this simulation, students start with $200 in their bank accounts and then explore what happens, over 25 years, if the account earns a constant interest at rates of 1% each year, 5% each year, or 10% each year. The simulation's Control Panel was illustrated earlier in this lesson.

1. Using the Computer Simulation to Explore How Interest Works

For each situation, students record information in a Table; expected results are shown below.

If the interest rate is:	Interest Earned: Year 1?	Year 10?	Year 25?	Total Interest Earned: Full 25 Years
1% each year?	$2.00	$2.19	$2.54	$56.49
5% each Year?	$10.00	$15.51	$32.25	$477.27
10% each Year?	$20.00	$47.16	$196.99	$1966.94

2. Putting the Pieces Together

A. Students are asked to write at least 2 observations about the interest income they earned over the 25 years with hints to look for patterns as they move across the columns (hint 1, below) and up and down the rows (hint 2, below) of the Table.

1. In all cases, more interest is earned each year as the 25 years progress. This is the result of the Reinforcing Feedback Loop: adding interest to the account makes the account bigger, which earns more interest the next year, which makes the account still bigger, so that your savings grow ever-faster with time.
2. As the interest rate increases, so too does the Interest Earned and that increase is not proportional to the increased interest rate. Note above that doubling the interest rate from 5% to 10% results in about **5 times** as much interest income over the 24 years.

B. Students are also challenged to use a Stock and Flow Map (with an added Connector from the Stock to the Flow) and a new tool, a Causal Loop Diagram, to explain what is happening with the compounding interest. Both tools provide means to describe a Reinforcing Feedback Loop and each tells essentially the same story.

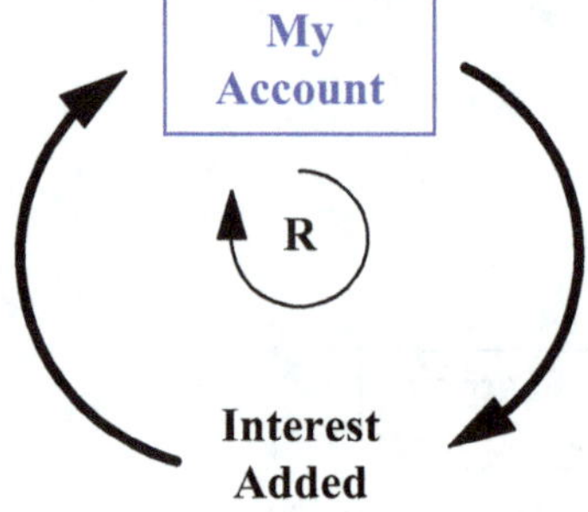

For the Causal Loop Diagram, note that the arrow on the right side (moving from MY ACCOUNT to Interest Added) serves the same purpose as the skinny arrow in the Stock and Flow Map; the arrow on the left side (from Interest Added to MY ACCOUNT) serves the same purpose as the Flow in the Stock and Flow Map.

Where and When Will Students Need Guidance?

1. Fully understanding the mathematics behind the process of compounding is likely to be beyond the grasp of many, although we tried to keep it as simple as possible by working with illustrations that used whole numbers in Exercise 1. As such, the simulation (as in the earlier conceptual exercise) is designed to help students learn by observing an unfamiliar pattern of behavior and asking better questions. Compounding, in general, is not beyond their means to understand. Students need to be comfortable with the basics in understanding why compounding growth is not linear: because the amount of growth is influenced by the size of the STOCK. Thus, as the STOCK grows, it leads to greater growth, a still larger STOCK and still greater growth....
2. Interpreting Graphs: Students should be able both to interpret and (in the first exercise) to create Graphs illustrating Behavior-over-Time.
3. Computer games can focus all too often on "Winning." The purpose in using this simulation is to be able to compare PLANS and their implications. It recognizes a range of options (e.g., looking for higher interest rates and keeping one's money in a savings account for a long time) to reap the greater benefits of larger interest payments.

Bringing the Lesson Home

? What is the important student-learning from these exercises and this simulation?

- *Interpreting Graphs: Students work with Behavior-over-Time Graphs and should recognize their value for illustrating compounding or exponential growth.*
- *Understanding how compounding works, not only within a financial context (compound interest) but also in a number of broader settings.*
- *Applying these insights beyond the particular illustrations:Although the simulation does have a "best" answer (there is a particular strategy which yields the greatest amount of interest here), it is equally important that the student recognize the limits of this simulation in framing better questions: e.g., What are the trade-offs in long-term saving versus spending? What is a realistic long-term interest rate? Learning can be most powerful when students think outside the box.*

Name____

How Does Compounding Work?

***The process of compounding growth is a part of our everyday lives.* Select one of the three illustrations below and, using the tools provided below (Table, Graph, Stock and Flow Map, and Causal Loop Diagram), describe what is happening in the story.**

1. Rumors: 1 person decides to start a rumor. Each day for 5 days, that person tells 1 other, each of whom, in turn, tells 1 other each day, each of whom tells 1 other each day, … and so on. How many people are spreading the rumor after 5 days?

2. Infection: A person becomes sick and remains sick for 5 days. Each day, that person infects 2 others; they each infect 2 others each day, each of whom infects 2 each day … and so on. How many sick people are there after 5 days?

3. An Offer You Can't Refuse: Your father offers you a choice; he will (1) give you $100 today, or (2) give you $1, and then each day for the next 5, he promises to add 2 dollars for every 1 you already have. Which is the better deal for you?

A. Calculate your answer. Use the Table and then present your answer on the appropriate Graph below.

Illustration 1:

Table

Days	STOCK	Daily Change
0	1	
1		
2		
3		
4		
Final		

Graph

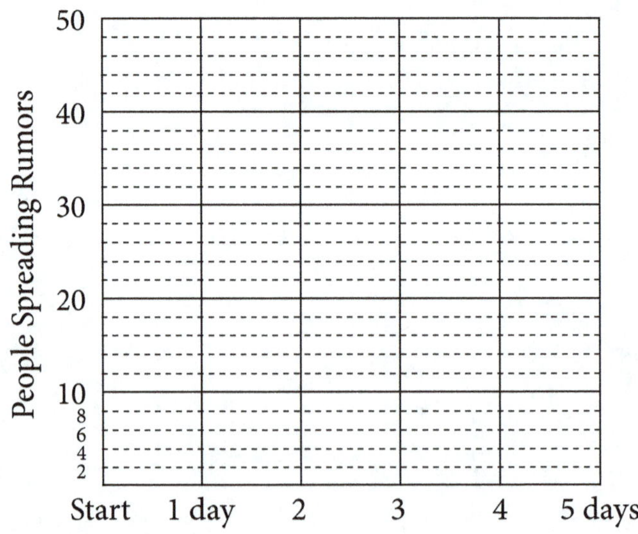

Illustration 2 or 3:

Table

Days	STOCK	Daily Change
0	1	
1		
2		
3		
4		
Final		

Graph

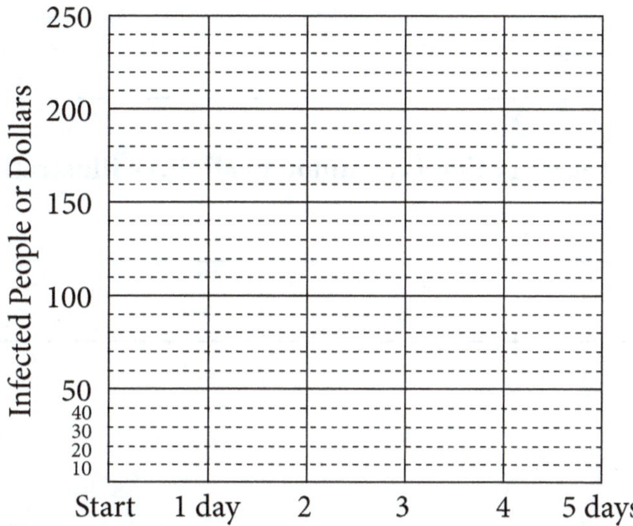

B. Tell the story using systems thinking.

Use the two diagrams below to help describe the system behind what is happening. In each case, select and insert the 2 key elements from your illustration (using the list to the right) in the appropriate space.

Key Elements Available

1. New Rumor Spreaders
2. People Become Ill
3. New Dollars for my Account
4. People Spreading Rumors
5. Sick People
6. My Dollars

Stock (S) and Flow (F) Map:

S:_______________

F:_______________

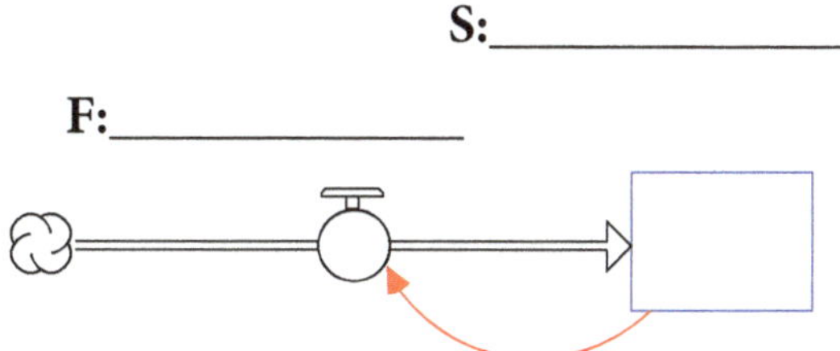

HINT: The skinny arrow indicates that the STOCK (whatever it contains) AFFECTS the Flow…

Causal Loop Diagram:

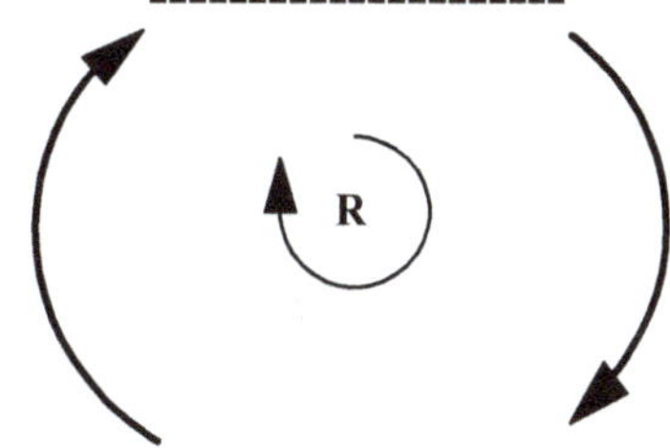

HINT: The two arrows indicate that one element CAUSES a change in the other element; that change, in turn, CAUSES the first element to change again. The "R" indicates this is a Reinforcing Feedback Loop; that means the original change (whether it is increasing or decreasing) is amplified each time you go around the loop.

Now tell the STORY (What is happening and WHY) in words.

____

____

C. What is the story that is common to all three illustrations?

____

____

Name____

Earning Interest On a Savings Account

Albert Einstein reputedly called compound interest "*the most powerful force in the universe.*" What did he mean by this? Let's explore…

You now have a real bank savings account, opened with $200 (perhaps a gift!). Each year the bank pays you interest on the amount of money in your account. That interest is then added to your account. What this means is the interest the bank will pay you on your account next year will build on the interest the bank has already paid you. Each year you get more interest than the year before. Pretty neat!

1. Use the computer simulation to explore how interest works.
Start with $200 in your account. See what happens over 25 years, if your account earns interest rates of 1% each year, 5% each year, or 10% each year.

For each situation, record information in the Table below.

If the interest rate is:	Interest Earned: Year 1?	Year 10?	Year 25?	Total Interest Earned: Full 25 Years
1% each year?				
5% each Year?				
10% each Year?				

2. Briefly answer the following questions using the information from the Table.
Write at least 2 observations about the interest you earned over the 25 years. (HINT: Look for patterns as you move across, as well as up and down, in the table above.)

A. ____

B. ____

3. What do you notice about the amount of money you received in interest when the interest rate doubled from 5% to 10%? (Hint: Did the amount of interest you receive double?)

____

____

Name____

4. Explaining how interest works. Can you explain to someone else what happened with interest in your bank account?

A. We would like you to tell the story by first labeling the Stock and Flow Map below.

1. What is the STOCK that is accumulating?
2. What is flowing in to add to that accumulation?

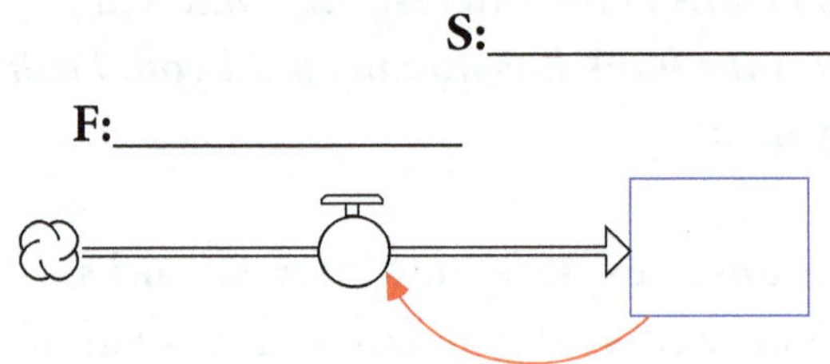

B. Next, add the "compounding" part of the interest story. The red arrow says something in the STOCK caused something to happen to the Flow. What caused what to happen?

____

____

C. Another way to describe what is happening uses a Causal Loop Diagram. Note that the diagram contains two arrows to create a closed loop. Can you use this to describe what is causing what to happen to MY ACCOUNT and Interest Added? When does it stop?

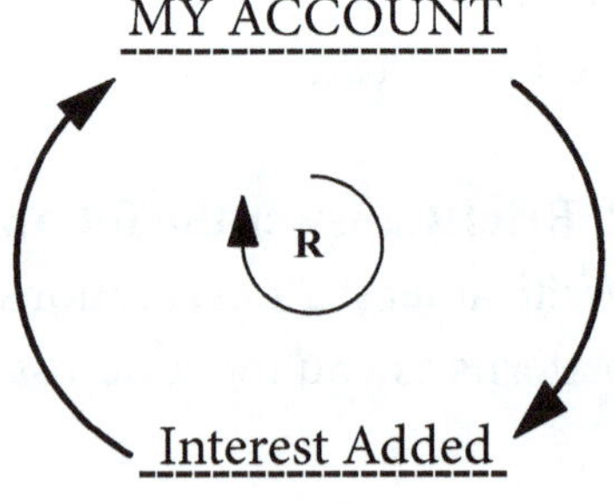

____

____

Lesson 7

Can Compounding Interest Make Me a Millionaire?

Instructions for Teachers

Student Challenge:

This culminating lesson brings together all of the concepts developed in earlier lessons (saving, spending, and compounding interest) to offer students a real-world challenge to save $1 million. Using a computer simulation, students are challenged to see if (and how) an average person, starting an everyday job at age 21, can manage this ambitious personal financial GOAL within a period of 44 years (their working lives!) or less.

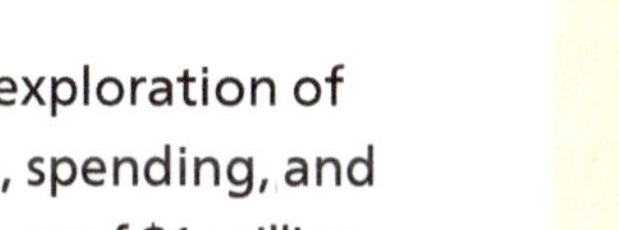

At the Lesson's End:

- Students will have completed a structured exploration of the connections between long-term saving, spending, and compounding interest in generating a net savings of $1 million.
- Students will have used tables, graphs, and systems thinking concepts to select and evaluate different saving and spending strategies, together with different interest rates; to identify their preferred PLANS based on personal values; and to share their results with classmates (and parents!).

(See the following Instructions and the Worksheet for more details)

NOTE

The material developed in Lesson 1 and Lesson 6 is strongly recommended to familiarize students with the basic concepts that are used and further expanded in this lesson.

MATERIALS

- Computer Simulation (available on-line at http://clexchange.org/curriculum/dollarsandsense/lesson7.asp).
- Worksheet to record plans and results.

Overview

Lesson 7 contains a single exercise, utilizing a computer simulation, to allow students to explore the implications of long-term efforts, reflected in saving, spending, and interest rates, to accumulate $1 million. Prior to using the simulation students are encouraged to work on paper to develop budgets (Income and Expenses) based on real-world salaries and costs.

The decisions the students make, together with various interest rates, are then entered into the simulation using the Control Panel. The Control Panel, reproduced below, shows 3 PLANS using a Fireman's salary of $2600/month, an Annual Interest Rate of 4%, and 3 different monthly Expenses: $2250, $2000, and $1750. NOTE: the success in PLAN #3 (Expenses of $1750) comes with considerable sacrifice in minimizing monthly Expenses!

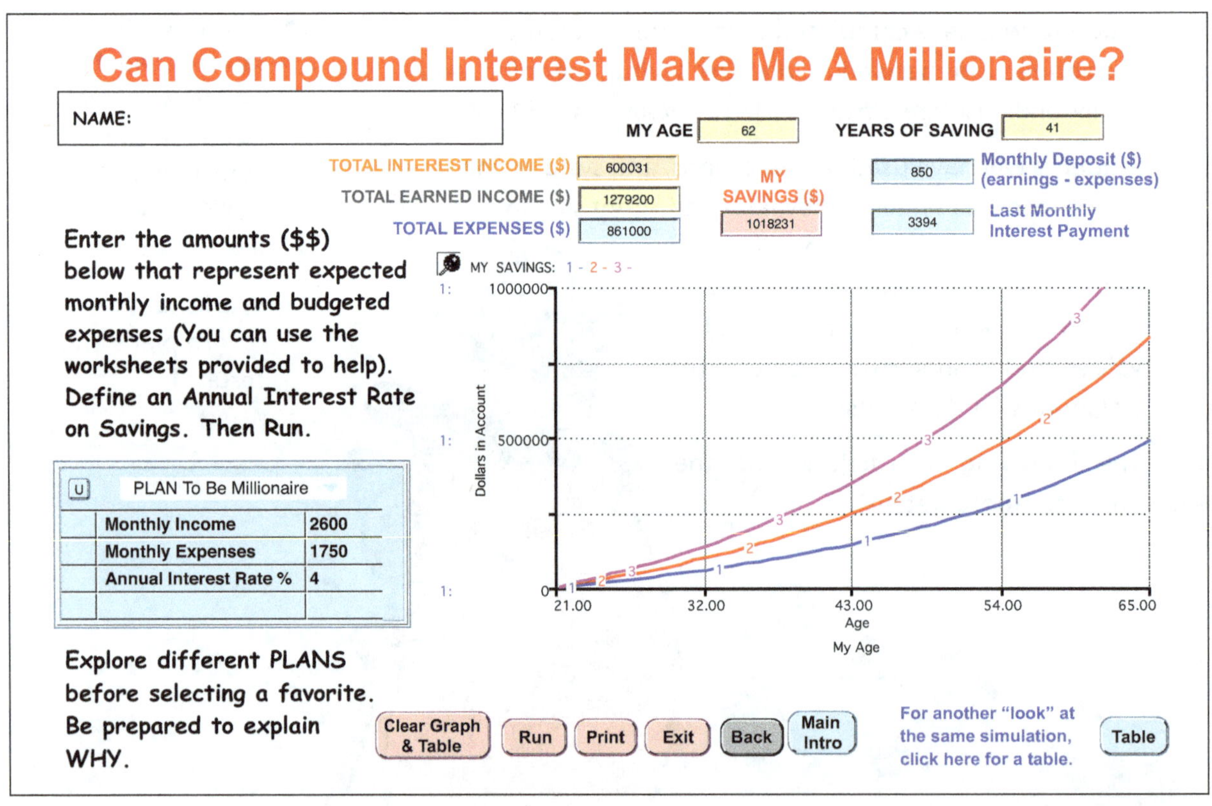

Students will observe that in these illustrations, the STOCK of MY SAVINGS grows at an ever-increasing rate. To understand what is behind that pattern of growth, it is critical to recognize three factors—all operating simultaneously—that contribute to the flow of money in and out of one's account.

1. Money flows into MY SAVINGS through two sources: Earnings Income <u>and</u> Interest Income. Money flows out in the form of Expenses. *The fact that MY SAVINGS consistently grows means that the two sources of Income always exceed Expenses. This reinforces a core principle for managing personal finance:* SPEND LESS THAN YOU EARN.
2. The Flow of Earnings Income into MY SAVINGS is constant in this illustration; hence, Earnings Income causes MY SAVINGS to grow steadily or linearly. That means the non-linear pattern of growth in MY SAVINGS reflects a changing amount of Interest Income.

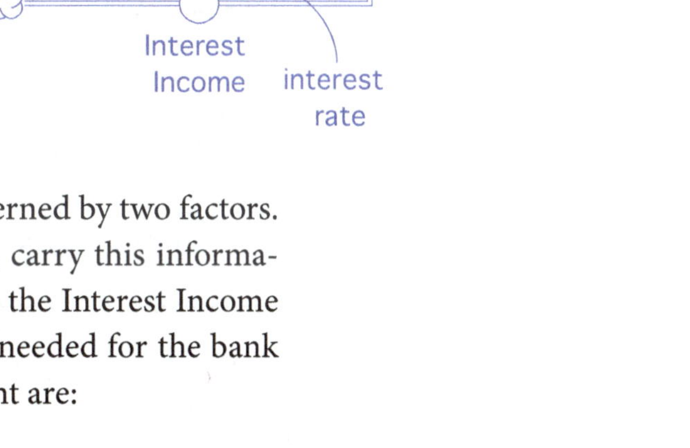

3. The amount of Interest Income (in blue, in the Stock and Flow Map), which the bank pays each year, is governed by two factors. Two "connectors," the skinny arrows, carry this information from other parts of the model to the Interest Income Flow. The two pieces of information needed for the bank to calculate its annual interest payment are:
   a. The amount of money in MY SAVINGS; and
   b. The interest rate paid by the bank.

The Interest Income is then added to MY SAVINGS. The next interest payment will be larger, since it will then be based on this larger amount in MY SAVINGS.

Compounding interest creates a Reinforcing Feedback Loop. Interest Income added to MY SAVINGS increases the amount of money in that STOCK, thus increasing the amount of interest received next year, resulting in still more money in MY SAVINGS . . . and so on.

If left alone for a long time, reinforcing feedback produces explosive growth.

Optional Pre-Lesson Discussion

Although Lesson 7 contains a single, simulation-based, exercise, prior to letting the students work with the simulation, we strongly recommend that students stop and think: How Much is $1 Million?

There are two ways to approach this question.

1. What Could You *Buy* with $1 Million?

Consider a few simple illustrations (or choose your own).

Item	Cost For One:	# You Could Buy with $1 Million:
House	$250,000	4
Car	$25,000	40
Family Trip to Disneyworld	$2500	400
Nintendo Wii	$250	4000
OTHER?		

2. How Long Would It Take an Average Working Person to Save $1 Million? (Assuming they only earned money but never spent any!)

Job and Hourly Pay	Total Hours to Earn $1 Million	Weeks to Earn $1 Million	Years to Earn $1 Million
Fast Food Counter Help ($8 an hour)	125,000	3125	62.5
Taxi Driver ($10 an hour)	100,000	2500	50
Postal Clerk ($25 an hour)	40,000	1000	20
OTHER?			

Note: If you would like students to learn about what different jobs pay, have them check the Bureau of Labor Statistics (*http://www.bls.gov/oes/2008/may/oes_nat.htm#b00-0000*).

Bringing The Lesson Home
(for the Pre-Simulation Exercise)

LEARNING

? What would be the greatest benefit of having $1 million?
Here's a chance to have students examine/communicate what they value most.

? How many fast food workers, taxi drivers, or postal clerks do you think are millionaires? Why do you think this?
The numbers shown don't factor in their normal living expenses —housing, transportation, food, etc. They need to pay for these out of their earnings. Therefore, it will take them even longer (much longer!) to save $1 million.

Lesson Structure

1. Planning—Developing a Budget on Paper

This simulation requires the students to identify their likely Income and Expenses. The worksheet provides guided instruction.

A. Developing a Budget: Income

Select a job from the options listed below. (The salaries are shown AFTER taxes have been taken out—students should be encouraged to ask a parent about that!)

	PAY AFTER TAXES	
JOB	ANNUAL	MONTHLY (rounded to nearest $10)
Teacher	$35,000	$2,920
Local TV Reporter	$32,000	$2,670
Fireman	$31,000	$2,580
Cook	$28,000	$2,330
Model (NOT *super*model)	$26,000	$2,170
Insurance Agent	$37,000	$3,090
Nurse	$48,000	$4,000
OTHER: ______________	$______	$_____

B. Developing a Budget: Expenses

Students are provided a range of options for their lifestyle and expenses. They are asked to describe them in the following way.

1. Circle the amount they choose to spend in each budget category.
2. Write that amount in the 3rd column.
3. Add the 6 amounts to arrive at their total monthly expenses.

Budget Category	Range of Monthly Expenses			Your Choice
HOUSING (with water, heat, and electricity)	$750 rent small apartment	$1000 rent comfy condo	$1500 buy a house	
TRANSPORTATION	$50 bus pass or old basic car	$250 own 3 yr old car	$450 drive new car	
ELECTRONICS (phone, computer, tv)	0 own none	$125 basic services	$250 all services	
FOOD	$200 basics	$350 good	$500 fancy	
ENTERTAINMENT	$100 basic	$200 moderate	$300 extensive	
OTHER EXPENSES	$150	$300	$500	
TOTAL EXPENSES =	Add all your expenses together OR pick one of the following summary values for total monthly expenses: Careful: $1250	Modest: $2225	Moderate: $3500	

To make sure students appreciate the choices they are making, they are asked to respond to this question: "Following a budget can be difficult. What sacrifice (or sacrifices), if any, will be the most challenging for you and why?" This offers a reality check for both students and teachers to reflect carefully on what it means to create and follow a budget (and, presumably, make trade-offs in the short-term to achieve longer-term benefits).

C. Selecting an Interest Rate for Savings

Banks over the years have paid interest rates on insured savings that range from VERY low (less than 1% per year) to relatively high (approaching 10% during inflationary times). We provide students with the opportunity to choose a rate from within that range and encourage them to experiment to see what effect different rates will have on their savings outcome.

2. Using the Computer Simulation—Asking "What Ifs"

The simulation provides an opportunity for students to test and revise(!) their PLANS over a 44-year (age 21 to 65) period. Will their PLANS generate the desired outcome ($1,000,000)? Students should devise and test several PLANS to explore different options. Those PLANS are recorded in a Table (illustrated below); the entries correspond to the information provided on the Control Panel shown earlier in this lesson.

	Choices			Results	
PLAN #	Monthly Earned Income ($ per month)	Monthly Expenses ($ per month)	Interest Rate on Savings (%)	Time to earn $1,000,000 (years)	OR Total $$ in MY SAVINGS (at age 65)
1	2600	2250	4	-	$484,734
2	2600	2000	4	-	$830,973
3	2600	1750	4	41 years	-

3. Using Graphs and Tables

Students use Graphs and Tables to describe and communicate the patterns of change that they observe over time in their accounts. (Tables and Graphs can be printed from the simulation or created by the students themselves.) Each has distinctive strengths.

- The Behavior-over-Time Graph in the simulation allows students to compare the 3 different PLANS identified earlier; the colors match the PLANS. Note that, of the three PLANS tested, only PLAN 3 (with perhaps painfully reduced expenses) is successful. (See illustration of the Control Panel earlier in these Instructions.)
- The Table records savings in MY SAVINGS changing as a result of additions of yearly income and new interest, as

well as subtractions of regular yearly Expenses. Notice how, in the case of the successful PLAN 3, as the account reaches $1 million (age = 62), the last year's "Interest Income" is almost FOUR TIMES GREATER (about $38,770 versus $10,200) than the added net earnings (Earned Income minus Expenses). This example illustrates the explosive power of compounding interest!

Years	MY SAVINGS	Expenses	Earned Income	Interest Income
51	$572,066.37	$21,000.00	$31,200.00	$22,882.65
52	$605,149.02	$21,000.00	$31,200.00	$24,205.96
53	$639,554.98	$21,000.00	$31,200.00	$25,582.20
54	$675,337.18	$21,000.00	$31,200.00	$27,013.49
55	$712,550.67	$21,000.00	$31,200.00	$28,502.03
56	$751,252.69	$21,000.00	$31,200.00	$30,050.11
57	$791,502.80	$21,000.00	$31,200.00	$31,660.11
58	$833,362.91	$21,000.00	$31,200.00	$33,334.52
59	$876,897.43	$21,000.00	$31,200.00	$35,075.90
60	$922,173.33	$21,000.00	$31,200.00	$36,886.93
61	$969,260.26	$21,000.00	$31,200.00	$38,770.41
Final	$1,018,230.67			

4. Putting the Pieces Together

A. After completing the exercise, students are asked to ANALYZE and DESCRIBE what happened and why. As part of their analysis, students should be able to recognize the following.

1. After some time had passed, the interest being earned was more than the income being earned (after expenses) and deposited each year. As the account got closer to $1,000,000, almost all the money moving into MY SAVINGS was from that interest! There really is an impressive "something for nothing" feeling to such compounding interest **IF** it is left to do its thing long enough!
2. The annual interest being earned by the time $1,000,000 is accumulated is (typically) MORE than the student's income. This concept opens up an area of discussion focused on the value of saving for retirement. If I build

up a large enough nest egg, can I stop working and meet my Expenses on the interest from MY SAVINGS?

B. Use a Graph and a Table to compare different options; to select from a number of successful options one's optimal PLAN; and to explain why the optimal PLAN was selected.

C. Work and communicate with others to compare observations and to recognize how the pieces of the puzzle work together. In the process of communicating with each other, students discover there are a number of ways to meet the PLAN GOAL of saving $1 million. Some are better than others, for different individuals; but there is no single right answer.

Where and When Will Students Need Guidance?

1. Fully understanding the mathematics behind the complex processes of saving, spending, **and** compounding interest can be beyond the grasp of many students. As such, this simulation is designed to help students think about real-world personal finance issues, including "average" salaries and monthly expenses, as they combine with compounding interest to generate unfamiliar (and impressive!) patterns of long-term savings.
2. Students should be comfortable with the "Basics," in understanding why compounding growth is not linear: because the amount of growth is influenced by the size of the STOCK. Thus, as the STOCK grows, it leads to greater growth, a still larger STOCK and still greater growth, and so on.
3. Computer games can focus all too often on "Winning." The purpose in using this simulation is to be able to compare PLANS and their implications, and to recognize the range of options on income (salaries), expenditures, and rates of interest. This simulation is designed to encourage students to explore those options and to evaluate important trade-offs. Each student needs to explicitly consider the following questions.

- *How do I set expenditures to match my desired "quality of life"?*
- *What trade-offs am I willing to make in the short term (e.g., living a more frugal lifestyle than I may want) to enjoy the longer-term advantages of having a million dollars?*
- *How can I maximize the return on my savings?*

Bringing the Lesson Home

? What is the important student-learning from this simulation?

- *Understanding and appreciating the importance of math in designing a financial plan to operate over an extended period of time; being successful exploring different strategies or plans; and understanding the utility of Graphs and Tables.*
- *Learning to compare, discuss, and even (respectfully and constructively) to disagree on their choices. Learning from one another is very powerful.*

Extending the Learning

This simulation offers opportunities for students to think about personal financial planning as a multi-faceted endeavor involving career (income) and lifestyle (expenses) choices and trade-offs. Ideally, this savings challenge will inspire questions about other large expense items (e.g., buy a home or save for college), both how to obtain them and what one needs to sacrifice in the short term to receive long-term benefits.

Name____

Can Compounding Interest Make Me a Millionaire?
Using the Simulation

Albert Einstein is said to have called compound interest "*the most powerful force in the universe.*" Is it powerful enough to make an average young adult (like you will soon be!) into a millionaire? This exercise gives you the chance to make a PLAN and use a computer simulation to explore ways that an average young adult might budget and save to BECOME A MILLIONAIRE!!

To use the simulation, you will need to record your expected monthly income, monthly expenses, and interest rate on savings. Steps 1–3 help guide you in making those 3 choices. Steps 4–5 help you evaluate your PLANS.

1. Developing a Budget: INCOME

Select your job from the options listed below. (The salaries are shown AFTER taxes have been taken out—ask a parent about that!)

Job	Annual	Monthly Pay After Taxes (rounded to nearest $10)
Teacher	$35,000	$2,920
Local TV Reporter	$32,000	$2,670
Fireman	$31,000	$2,580
Cook	$28,000	$2,330
Model (NOT *super*model)	$26,000	$2,170
Insurance Agent	$37,000	$3,090
Nurse	$48,000	$4,000
OTHER: _______________	$______	$_____

2. Developing a Budget: EXPENSES

On the Table below, do the following.

A. Circle the amount you choose to spend in each budget category.

B. Write that amount in the 3rd (YOUR CHOICE) column.

C. Add the 6 amounts to arrive at your TOTAL (monthly) EXPENSES.

Name____

Budget Category	Range of Monthly Expenses			Your Choice
HOUSING (with water, heat, and electricity)	$750 rent small apartment	$1000 rent comfy condo	$1500 buy a house	
TRANSPORTATION	$50 bus pass or old basic car	$250 own 3 yr old car	$450 drive new car	
ELECTRONICS (phone, computer, tv)	0 own none	$125 basic services	$250 all services	
FOOD	$200 basics	$350 good	$500 fancy	
ENTERTAINMENT	$100 basic	$200 moderate	$300 extensive	
OTHER EXPENSES	$150	$300	$500	
TOTAL EXPENSES =	Add all your expenses together <u>OR</u> pick one of the following summary values for total monthly expenses: Careful: $1250	Modest: $2225	Moderate: $3500	

Following a budget can be difficult. What sacrifice (or sacrifices), if any, will be the most challenging for you and why?

____

____

____

3. Selecting an INTEREST RATE on Savings

In addition to calculating income and expenses, you will need to **SELECT AN INTEREST RATE** that your savings will earn. NOTE: While there are many options for investing those savings in the "real world," many involve taking risks. Over the past 20 years, *safe* bank savings accounts and Certificates of Deposit (another kind of safe savings) **have paid on average 5% per year.** (See: *http://www.bankrate.com/brm/publ/passbkchart.asp.*)

Name____

4. Recording your Choices

Record your choices (Income, Expenses, Interest Rate) in the first three open columns of the Table below. Then, open the simulation, enter your information, and RUN the model. The model begins at age 21 and gives you up to 44 years (to age 65) to get your million dollars. **Record your results in the final two open columns of PLAN 1 in the worksheet.**

Try different options. Record your choices and results below for PLAN 2 and later PLANS. Keep trying until you are satisfied with your results, filling in new PLANS, as needed.

	Choices			Results	
Plan #	Monthly Earned Income ($ per month)	Monthly Expenses ($ per month)	Interest Rate on Savings (%)	Time to earn $1,000,000 (years)	OR Total $$ in MY SAVINGS (at age 65)
1					
2					
3					
4					
5					

5. Comparing and Contrasting PLANS to become a MILLIONAIRE

A. Prepare a Graph or a Table (or print from the simulation) that shows your favorite PLAN. Use it to explain why you chose this PLAN over other successful options.

____

____

____

B. Recognizing there are many ways to be successful, did you choose the "fastest way?" If not, why not? If so, can you identify why the fastest way might be harder to achieve than other PLANS?

____

____

____

About Us

The Creative Learning Exchange

The Creative Learning Exchange (CLE) is a non-profit organization in Acton, Massachusetts dedicated to promoting learner-centered learning and system dynamics in K-12 education. The CLE disseminates classroom curricular materials developed by teachers, publishes a quarterly newsletter, hosts a biennial conference for educators and interested citizens, maintains a listserve, and provides system dynamics training materials and programs for educators. Information is available at *www.clexchange.org*.

System Dynamics

System dynamics is a field of study and a perspective for understanding change. Using computer simulation and other tools, system dynamics looks at how the feedback structure of systems causes the change we observe all around us. System dynamics was developed fifty years ago by Professor Jay W. Forrester at MIT and is used to address problems in areas ranging from ecology, to business management, economics, and psychology. Under Forrester's guidance, system dynamics is helping teachers make K-12 education more learner-centered, engaging, challenging and relevant to our rapidly changing world.

CLE Curriculum Series

This series of books, *Dollars and Sense, The Shape of Change* and *The Shape of Change: Stocks and Flows,* introduces students and their teachers to some of the basic ideas of system dynamics and systems thinking as a way to observe and understand change.

MORE INFORMATION AVAILABLE:

Dollars and Sense I and II,
The Shape of Change *and*
The Shape of Change: Stocks and Flows

on the
Creative Learning Exchange at:

www.clexchange.org

These lessons and their handouts, as well
as many others can be accessed
via the CLE website

www.ingramcontent.com/pod-product-compliance
Lightning Source LLC
LaVergne TN
LVHW081413110826
845149LV00010B/1728

* 9 7 8 0 9 9 6 0 1 2 8 0 5 *